TAXI TALES
AND OTHER STORIES

John Lockett

BROWN
DOG
BOOKS

Published under licence by Brown Dog Books and
The Self-Publishing Partnership, 7 Green Park Station,
Bath BA1 1JB

www.selfpublishingpartnership.co.uk

ISBN printed book: 978-1-78545-292-5
ISBN e-book: 978-1-78545-293-2

Cover design by Kevin Rylands
Internal design by Andrew Easton

Printed and bound in the UK

John Lockett standing by a mocked-up taxi in a recreated scene

The author would like to thank:

Henry Legg for the author's photo

Ellen Broom for cleaning up the Prague photo

Jay Maddison for the front cover drawing

Paul Gray for finding some more emails

Contents

Part 3 – **Motorcycle Stories**

Preface

This second volume of stories, from the four-and-a-half-year period when I drove a taxi in Scotland, are tales that I somehow missed, due in part to the sheer volume and frequency of incidents – or I just forgot about them. Hard to believe I could forget about some of these incidents, but I did, and I also had some of them on the 'back burner', as it were. I left them out of the first book, *Diary of a Taxi Driver*, because they were either incomplete or I couldn't recall key points, and some were omitted until I could disguise them sufficiently to protect certain individuals. There were also times when I had no internet or my old laptop would be out of service, which meant I couldn't email the latest incidents to my mother. I didn't bother to write them down either because at the time I never thought a book would result from all the wild, weird and wonderful occurrences.

Also, I never once thought that on 31 December 2016 a very good friend of mine would throw herself off a motorway bridge in an attempt to end her life. Thankfully, Alison survived the horror of what she had done, despite breaking almost every bone in her body, and that was the event that triggered me to actually compile the first book from the old emails. She was wrapped up like a mummy with numerous pipes and wires attached to her when I visited her in hospital after she finally regained consciousness a few weeks after that awful New Year's Eve, and she asked me, with great difficulty, to cheer her up. I told her one of my taxi stories and she then asked me to promise I would write them all down for her to read while she underwent her long road to rehabilitation. It was at that moment I decided to write a book. I'm glad to say that Alison has now made an amazing recovery from her horrific injuries and is well on the way to full health.

While I was writing that first book, my mind was totally focussed on it and nothing else. There were other factors I won't go into here that meant I edited and released it quite speedily, although I should also add not hastily. I put everything I could into it and I hope I created something that people can enjoy. Once I had started editing and polishing those initial emails into *Diary of a Taxi Driver*, my mind blanked out all other stories. However, within a few days of that book being published, the tales that had remained hidden slowly started to come back. Paul, a great friend of mine, found a document that he'd made from other emails I had lost, and that helped enormously, too.

Unlike the first book, the chapters here have no date in the title. However, due to the circumstances of most of the incidents, the shift I was working, or even the persons in the taxi at the time, I have managed to put the chapters into a fairly logical timeline. The first few incidents occurred on night shift so they start the book off, then the bulk of the stories form the middle of the book. Ending the book are tales that, because of their nature, I know happened towards the later months of my taxi-driving career.

The last part of this book contains just two chapters which have nothing to do with taxi driving whatsoever. They are motorcycle stories. One chapter concerns the most amazing holiday in Europe on a motorcycle I ever had in 1993. The other relays stories about when some friends and I engaged in very low budget motorcycle racing between 1995 and 2000. I hope you enjoy them.

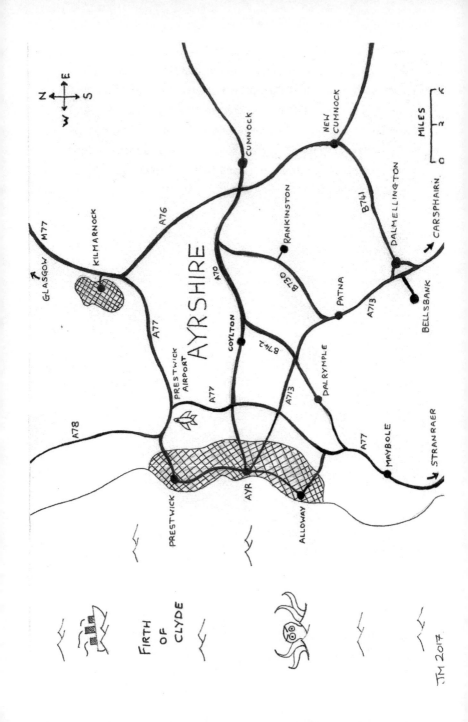

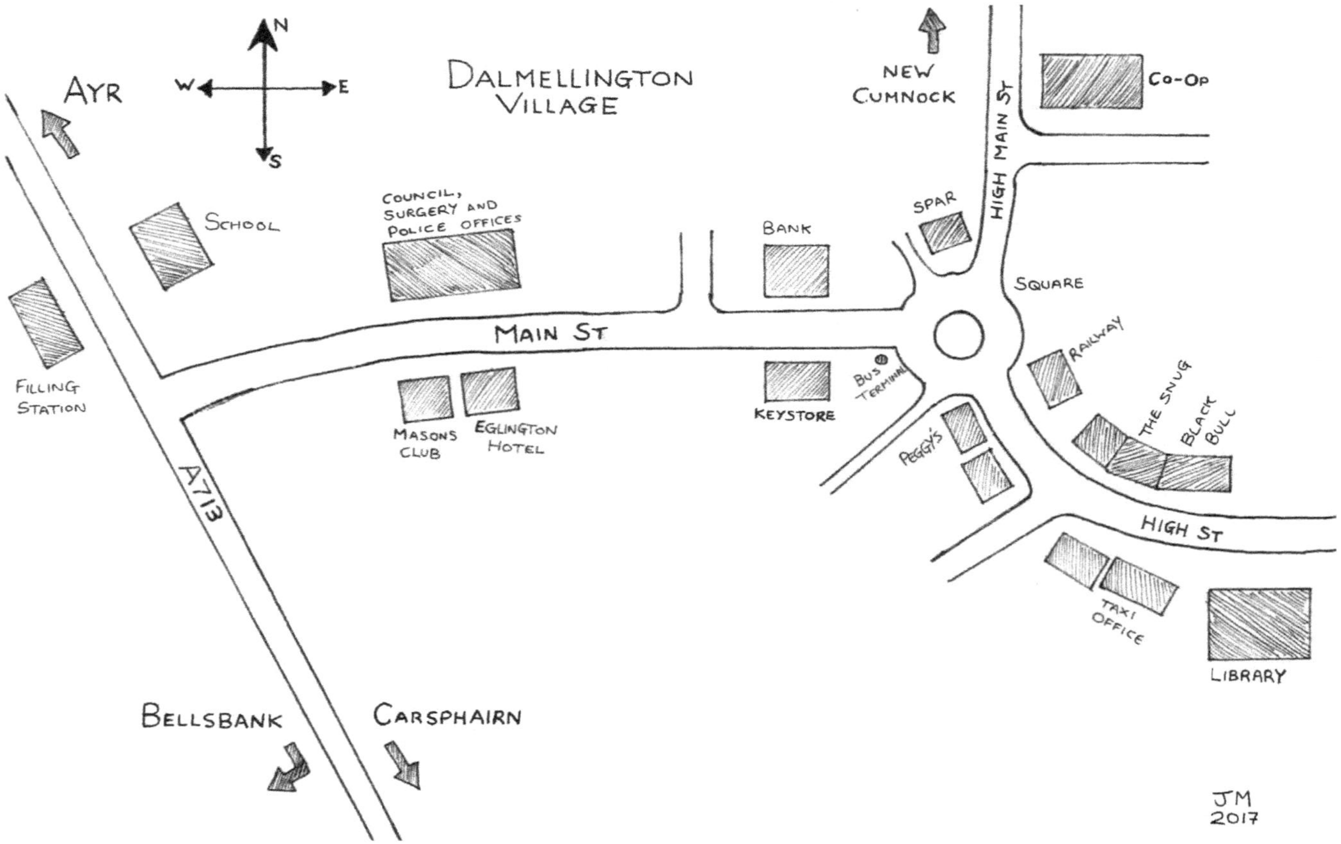

Dalmellington Village

AYR

NEW CUMNOCK

Co-Op

HIGH MAIN ST

SQUARE

RAILWAY

THE SNUG

BLACK BULL

HIGH ST

LIBRARY

TAXI OFFICE

PEOPLES

SPAR

BANK

Bus Terminus

KEYSTORE

COUNCIL, SURGERY AND POLICE OFFICES

MAIN ST

SCHOOL

EGLINGTON HOTEL

MASONS CLUB

FILLING STATION

A713

BELLSBANK

CARSPHAIRN

N W E S

JM 2017

PART ONE – INTRODUCTION

The Driver

My name is John, and for nearly five years from November 2006 to July 2011 I drove a taxi, or, more correctly, a private hire vehicle in Ayrshire, Scotland. I was born in 1963 in Birmingham and moved to Dalmellington in 2006 for a variety of reasons. Driving a taxi was originally only a stopgap job. That 'stopgap' lasted almost five years. It was a time when I met some truly great people and made some genuine friends. Oh yes, I also had some very interesting encounters, which really is the whole point of this book. Of the hires I did, 99 per cent were incident-free, and the overwhelming majority of people I met were the nicest folk you could wish to meet.

My previous occupations were nearly all warehousing jobs, driving fork trucks of varying kinds, which I actually enjoyed. Cars never interested me and still don't. I much prefer motorcycles. But when I got the opportunity to learn to drive a car and take my driving test in 1991, I did. I thought it would come in handy one day, and I was right. I often got asked to drive company pool cars to places around the country and work offsite. The driving didn't interest me at all but seeing new places and meeting new people did.

After I'd moved three hundred miles from where I'd always lived, it soon became necessary for me to earn some extra money until my own business started in earnest. I wanted something local so I went to a convenient job centre – that is, one of the local pubs. I bought a drink and scanned the room. My eyes settled on a guy who looked friendly enough and pretty soon we started up a conversation about this and that. I told him everything about myself and that I was looking for a part-time job. He suggested I try the taxi office round the corner, so I finished my squash and went for a very informal job interview with the boss of one of the village's two taxi outfits, the other being run by a chap called Andy. Boss was a no-nonsense kind of guy in his fifties. He ran a private hire business with about three cars and a van of some sort, and he needed a driver.

I had a lengthy chat with him and we got on right away. He gave me some pointers and a map of the village to help with my revising for the exam, which he arranged for me. A week later I passed my taxi driver test in Kilmarnock. It consisted of getting more than fifteen questions about local streets, routes and landmarks correct out of twenty. I scored seventeen, which, considering I'd only lived in the village a short while, wasn't too bad. I also passed the strict background checks that East Ayrshire Council utilised to weed out unsavoury sorts, and, combined with the fact I had a full and clean UK driving licence I soon had my taxi badge and was ready for business.

The Taxi

Strictly speaking, I drove a private hire vehicle or 'minicab', although I took the taxi driver test which entitled me to drive a taxi *or* PHV (private hire vehicle). A PHV test means you can only drive a PHV, *not* a taxi. Both tests are the same and cost the same. None of that made any sense at the time and it doesn't now, to be honest. At the time I drove, the test and badge cost around £150 for three years, and the badge was renewable at the same cost every three years thereafter.

The main (and only apparent) difference between a taxi and a PHV is that taxis can ply for trade and pick up off the street and no name needs to be given to the driver. A person sticks their hand out as they see a taxi approaching or walks up to one on a taxi rank and gets in and the driver takes them where they want to go.

A PHV cannot ply for trade or pick up off the street. It must be booked in advance, usually via a phone call, or through a regular arrangement and a hirer's name obtained. I believe there are some technical differences too in relation to insurance and MOTs... etc. I never really got bogged down in the minutiae of the job, just the matters that directly affected me. Occasionally I would get a regular flag me down like I was a taxi and I would stop and pick them up if I had nothing on at that minute. There was no way I would drive past one of my regulars, especially in the rain.

However, if there had been taxis operating in the village, they would doubtless have complained that I had picked fares up off the street, complained to the council and I would have been in some bother or other. But as it was I never had bother off anyone. The difference between a taxi and PHV to the fare-paying customer isn't apparent anyway. Customers would always phone up and ask for a 'taxi'. In all the years I drove a PHV, only one person ever asked for a private hire vehicle, which actually confused me at the time, and they were American. Everyone, including the local council, called our vehicles 'taxis'.

The Village

Dalmellington and Bellsbank are very hilly communities. Dalmellington was the hub of the village, with a bank, surgery, council offices, numerous pubs as well as shops… etc. Bellsbank was an estate or 'scheme' at the end of one road to the south with a bar and a few shops. The job was mainly a case of taking senior ladies to the shops or doctors, a few old boys to the old folks' home for tea with their friends or the pub for some booze, and a hectic spate of school kids in the morning and mid-afternoon. There were numerous hires to Prestwick and Glasgow airports, too. I enjoyed nearly every hire I had, except for a handful of incidents that you'll read about later.

Boss instructed me in some basics about the village, certain characters I might encounter, rules and various other bits of information including the fact that most of the pubs in the village were known by completely different names to the one on the sign outside. The Railway, Peggy's and The Black Bull were nicknames for the three main pubs in Dalmellington, and I quickly committed these important details to memory. The Snug was the only pub in the village that didn't have an alternate name and doesn't actually feature at all in the following tales.

It closed not long after I started, too. Boss explained that the alternate names were old ones that the locals still used. Boyd's Bar had about three old names but for clarity I use only its latest here.

There are about thirty or so roads in Dalmellington and Bellsbank, with one road having an alternate name, one stretch of road having four names and another road having two names (with one of those names being almost identical to another road). There was one road that was actually three roads, and there was one house that was in a different road to the road in its address. Phew! Isn't town planning wonderful? Within a short space of time I had a map of the village in my head and the job became far easier than the hectic first few days proved to be.

The Office

The taxi office was a motley collection of chairs and a sofa in the waiting area, a wee kitchen and an office which consisted of higgledy piggledy paperwork, a landline phone (which we would divert to a mobile phone if working solo) and the taxi radio. Whoever worked the office radio was known as Control, and the drivers had a radio call sign code of their own and we could all hear each other no matter who was speaking to who.

Boss, radio call sign 'TC1', gave me the call sign 'TC6' to use on the taxi radio and liked to converse "properly" on it, so it was a case of "Roger" and "Over and out" most of the time. One of the more interesting radio codes that Boss utilised was that if we needed to answer the call of nature then we were to use the code name 'Mr Brown' over the radio. We both knew what it meant, but none of our passengers would, and since, unusually, there was no-one in the village with that name, it worked very well for us. It particularly came in useful during the 'Great Broken Toilet' fiasco that we endured for a few weeks until a suitable plumber could be located. Apart from people's names, which I have changed to something like 'Fred' or 'Mrs B' for obvious reasons, everything else is accurate. Names such as Mr Soandso or Soandso Street are used where I need to use the name of a person or street without accidentally using another real name or street. All fares are correct at the time the hire occurred.

On the subject of words, in the following tales I may occasionally use local words such as:

aye for yes

ken for know

pish for nonsense

blootered for drunk

brae for hill

messages for grocery shopping

and, of course, wee for small, little or tiny

PART TWO – TAXI TALES

Impossibly Confused Frustration

We all get a wee bit confused or forgetful from time to time. Confusion is most likely to happen in the first few weeks of taxi driving when you're new to the job, you may not know every street as well as you should, and you've got screaming and shouting punters in the car. The laminated A4-sized map of the village I'd made myself turned what could have been panic every time I was shouted over the radio into a relatively straightforward drive to a pick-up point. I marked key house numbers and other useful info on it for easy reference and it helped enormously. After a few weeks I didn't need it at all, so it spent a number of months in the door pocket before eventually disappearing. I still kept a street atlas of every community in Ayrshire in the glove box that was indispensable when doing parcel runs or hires outside the village, but I never used it to look at Dalmellington because I knew where everywhere was after a while.

A few weeks into the job, as I pulled up outside the office late one evening after Natalie had given me the all clear from the previous hire, she shouted me over the radio. Boss was elsewhere in the village.

Natalie – Control to TC6

Me – TC6 here. Go ahead

Natalie – What's your position, TC6? I've got a hire for you

Me – I've just pulled up outside the office

Natalie – Great. Go to the end of New Street and get Mr D. He's going to Ayr. He says he's stood outside his house. Easy enough to find

Me – Err... Roger

I hadn't heard of New Street. How can this be?! I'd been everywhere by now. Surely this was a joke. Yes, of course it is! I'm from Birmingham, and Natalie and Boss have come up with some lame ruse to send me on a wild goose chase. New Street railway station in my home city probably gave them the idea.

Me – TC6 to Control

Natalie – Go ahead, TC6

Me – Err... New Street. Where's that then?

Natalie – Jeez! It's right in front of you, TC6

Boss came over the radio now.

Boss – TC1 to TC thicko

Me (fed up) – Go ahead, TC1

Boss (laughing) – It's not the one in Birmingham. It's right in front of you if you're parked outside the office and facing the square

Where was this invisible street? I flicked the car's interior light on and got my wee street atlas out. No New Street to be found. My headlights were on and I looked ahead. The alleyway down the side of office just sat there doing nothing. Next along the street is an old storage building, then Peggy's pub and then the square itself. Bloody hell, where was it?

Natalie – You still outside, TC6?

Me – Err... Yes, I am

Within about twenty seconds Natalie strode out the office and past me towards the wee alleyway that went to... Actually, I didn't know where it went. I eased the car forward about ten yards and wound the window down. Pulling up next to Natalie in a state of confusion, she leant in the car and pointed down the alleyway I had never explored before. I just assumed it went nowhere and no-one lived down there.

Natalie – That's New Street, John

Me – What? That silly wee alleyway that doesn't go anywhere?

Natalie – That "silly wee alleyway" actually goes to the Bowling Club

Me – Oh right. I've never been down there. I go to the Bowling Club down Cathcartston

Natalie – Now you ken the back way. Go and get Mr D anyway

I pulled away and crawled along New Street, found Mr D who was stood outside one of the three houses at the end of the tight road and took him to Ayr. Needless to say, it was a source of embarrassment for me when I met up with Boss later, but it illustrated a point about me thinking I knew where everywhere was when I clearly didn't.

The months and years rolled by and I went from thinking I knew where everywhere was, to not only knowing the entire geography of the area but also its history and people and a lot more besides. I liked the vast majority of people I met, and although I find driving a car to be quite boring, I never really thought about it too much and just did it. Some jobs are like that. Drive the bloody taxi and take people where they need to go. Simple, really.

I picked a guy up in Bellsbank one Sunday afternoon and took him to the Running Dog pub in nearby Burnton. It would have been one of those hires that faded in the memory within minutes except for the moment we arrived and he paid me.

Guy – Is this place open?

Me (uninterested) – I don't think so. Not sure, to be honest

Guy – Hold on

He got out the car and went to the door of the pub, which he couldn't open, peered through a window and I could see him suddenly look very annoyed. The pub was clearly not open for business. He walked back to the taxi and got in.

Guy – It's not fuckin' open!

Me – Oh

Guy – Why didn't you tell me the place was closed?

Me – Is that my job? I drive this taxi mate. Anyway, for all I know you could be the guy who opens the pub up. You could work here

Guy – Don't be ridiculous. Why isn't it open?

Me – Now you're being ridiculous. You expect me to know why it's not open?

Guy – Now you're being awkward

Me – Oh, am I? Anyway, what do you want to do now?

Guy – Well, there's no point me staying here, is there?

Me – That's not really my decision to make, is it, Sir? I need to get off though. I've got other stuff to do

Guy – Take me to the Black Bull. Is it open?

Me – I think it is, but again, like I said before, it's not my job to worry about whether a place is open or not. My job is driving this silver Vauxhall Vectra and to take people where they ask me to. Is that clear? If I take you to the Bull, it's A) another hire you need to book in and pay for, and B) not my business if the pub is open or not. OK?

Guy (grumpily) – Aye, OK

I took the guy to the Bull, dropped him off and that was the end of that little scenario. I would do many favours for people over the years that weren't my job simply because I like helping others out. There was one senior lady I regularly took to the surgery, and I would put my hand under her shoe to assist her getting up the few steps back into her house. I read meters and took dustbins in from the roadside and all sorts of wee tasks and favours that weren't my job. I dropped a newspaper, a wee bottle of milk and a Freddo chocolate bar into another senior lady every Sunday morning when I worked the weekend day shifts, for reasons that Boss never explained and I never asked about. I just did it. The frustration would arise when people who weren't my gaffer asked me to do or know things that were clearly not my job, but they thought it was, or should be, or they would behave like I didn't have anything else to do besides worry about their pish. I never had any other hires to go and do according to their thinking, or rather their lack of thinking.

Impossible tasks were expected on a number of occasions, too. A regular customer who lived in the furthest street from the taxi office phoned up one day asking for a taxi "now". I told him I had nothing else on at that moment, would drive over immediately and be with him in a couple of minutes. "Not good enough," he told me. I explained that I didn't have a taxi capable of transporting through time and space instantaneously, but my witty retort fell on unreceptive ears.

A fairly busy weekend evening was speedily heading into oblivion when I was sent to a house in Bellsbank to pick up a lady. I pulled up outside and it seemed to take her forever to exit her house and get in the taxi. She looked all flustered and panicky and kept rummaging through her bag. I pulled away and hadn't even got to the junction at the end of her street fifty yards away when she shouted out.

Lady – Shit! I've left my mobile at home

Me – Oh

Lady – Can you go back?

I rounded the wee block of streets she lived on and pulled up outside her house once more. She clambered out and sprinted up the pathway back into her house. I was frustrated because I had a ten-minute clear spell after the hire which I intended to fill up with a quick dash back to the office for a fresh coffee and cigarette. The lady eventually emerged from her house, locked up with immense difficulty and almost threw herself back in the car. I pulled away thinking at least I had time for a quick microwaved coffee and a few quick puffs on a cigarette. Once again, I neared the junction at the end of her street.

Lady – Shit!

Me – What's up?

Lady – I forgot to pick something up. A wee present for my friend. Can you...?

Me – ...go back?

Once again, I swung round the wee block she lived on and we successfully wasted all the time it would have taken for me to grab a coffee and a smoke. It was frustrating rather than annoying, and I learned to ask certain folks if they had "phone, money, keys and anything else" with them as I picked them up. I saved me a few more wasted trips around the block over the years.

Towels

As regular as clockwork, every Sunday evening when I first started taxi driving I took a nice old guy called Frazer home from the Black Bull. He only ever said "hello" to me when he got in the cab, and "goodnight, John" when he got out. He never gave me any bother and was always ready when I went to collect him, so consequently I liked him and he was my first regular customer during those first weeks and months of night shift.

Boss would sometimes take him home depending on which of us was around at the time, but I usually got the shout while Boss attended to office chores. One evening as the usual time to take Frazer home neared, I was dozing off in a fairly uncluttered armchair while Boss sat behind a quivering tower of paperwork.

Boss (laughing) – Wake up, Lockett, you lazy herbert. Go and take Frazer home, and make sure you put this on the seat before he sits down

He threw a hand towel over to me. I caught it and tucked it under my arm.

Boss – You ken why I want him to sit on a towel?

Me – I can guess, Boss

Boss – I took him home last Sunday if you remember and he had an 'accident'. Hopefully the towel will prevent any more

I folded the towel over and put it on the seat for Frazer to sit on. I never said anything when he got in the taxi that evening, and neither did he. He looked at it before sitting down and I could tell he knew why it was there. I folded the towel over to double its thickness and there was no accident at all, but often times there was. For the next few weeks, this arrangement worked well, and the towel, once it had been 'used' was thrown in a plastic bag and laundered ready for next week.

The weeks passed and the single towel, even when folded over, became insufficient to prevent the seat upholstery getting wet, so Boss bought another hand towel and we folded both over. There were now four layers between Frazer and the seat, but after another few months even that wasn't enough. I rolled into the office on a Friday evening to start my shift.

Boss – Evening John

Me – Hi Boss

I put the kettle on while Boss explained what happened the previous Sunday night when he took Frazer home.

Boss – I've got some sad news, John

Me – Oh. What's up?

Boss – I took Frazer home last Sunday because you were off doing that hire from the airport. We got to his house, and instead of him paying me, getting out and going home with just a wee "goodnight Boss" he lifted the towels up. There was a wet patch on the upholstery about as big as a ten pence piece. He said, "sorry Boss" and then he lifted the towels out. He said, "I can't carry on like this Boss. Thank you, and John, for being so understanding and helpful about all this, but I think I'll stop going down the pub." He took the towels away with him and gave me a tenner to cover them

Me – Bloody hell. Poor guy. I'm pretty cut up about that

Boss – Me too, John. Frazer is a lovely bloke and I think we did the best we could for him, ourselves and other customers. But I don't think we'll see him again

I never did see Frazer again. If the guy had been drinking huge quantities of beer all night and getting absolutely blootered out of his head, then Boss wouldn't have put up with it for a week or two, never mind months. We knew for a fact that Frazer only had a pint or two with friends. Boss wanted to help the guy have his social Sunday night drink, but the old boy decided he just couldn't do it anymore.

Knife

Boss shouted me over the radio late one Saturday evening well after the pubs had closed. It was actually about 2am on the Sunday morning and I had just dropped off a nice couple in Bellsbank and was pootling back to the office through the deserted streets. It had been a fairly average night and I wasn't expecting any more hires at the time it was.

Boss – TC1 to TC6

Me – Go ahead, TC1

Boss – OK listen up well, TC6. There are two young lads wanting a taxi to Patna. I ken them both. They're OK but the one lad can be a bit of an idiot. He's called Peanut. The decent lad's name is McMinnar. They're stood opposite the junction of Merrick and Reicawr. You ken the routine by now

Me – OK, TC1. I'll be there in two minutes

I drove the short distance I was from the pick-up point and could easily see two young lads. One looked a regular lad in his late teens and the other youth had a weird-looking hoodie on. I pulled up next to them and wound the passenger window down.

McMinnar – This taxi for McMinnar?

Me – Aye it is. Get in, lads. Patna, isn't it?

McMinnar – Aye, pal

After I popped the door locks McMinnar sat in the front, with the guy I assumed to be Peanut taking the back seat. I pulled off and we were soon heading for Patna down the empty A713.

Me – Good night out tonight, lads?

McMinnar – Aye. We were just at a mate's house watching a movie and having a few beers

Peanut – Aye. If anyone messes with me they've had it, I tell you

Me – Who's messing with you?

Peanut – Just saying. Anyone messes with me. I'll sort them out

Me – Good. I'd sort anyone out who messed with me too. I think anyone would

Peanut – Yeah, well, I'd sort them out real good. You ken?

McMinnar – Bloody hell, Peanut. Shut up man

Peanut – Well I'm just saying to the driver, you ken, that I'd sort anyone out who messes with me

Me – I haven't messed you about, Sir

Peanut (looking smug) – Didn't say you had

By now we were ambling through Waterside and I picked up the pace a wee bit. This Peanut character was very unnerving. His hoodie had a low peak on it which had a kind of visor attached. I've never seen anything similar since and can't imagine what if any practical use it was. He was sat forward so his face was between the two front seats, and his voice was very grating.

Me – Oh well, that's cool. I never mess my customers about. I look after...

Peanut – I've got a knife if anyone messes with me

McMinnar – Fuck's sake man!

Now, this guy sounded serious and I was genuinely concerned. What do I do? Pull over in the approaching lay-by? Carry on and ignore him? Tell him to stop being so silly? I thought about lamping the brakes on. McMinnar was belted in but Peanut hadn't bothered putting his on. I couldn't see his hands and I decided I didn't want him flying through the car with what could be a knife in one of them that could harm either McMinnar or myself.

Me – I'll tell you something now, my friend, and I'm one hundred percent serious about this

Peanut (glancing at me with a grin on his face) – Go on, pal

Me – If anyone messes with you, they'll have me to answer to. You are my customer. I look after my customers. Therefore, if anyone gives you any pish I will not be very happy about it. I will "sort them out". Understand?

Peanut sat back and I could see McMinnar visibly relax. We entered Patna.

Peanut – You're alright you are, pal

Me – Just doing my job, Sir

I dropped them off at their destination and McMinnar paid me while Peanut slunk off up the pathway to the house messing with the visor thing on his hoodie.

McMinnar – Sorry about him, pal. He can be a right clown sometimes

Me – Not a problem, Sir

I drove back to base shaking very slightly until I reached the sanity of the office. A much-needed fresh coffee and a few cigarettes later I met up with Boss and, after a brief chat, drove home. I never saw Peanut again but I often saw McMinnar, who was a decent guy. I couldn't understand why they were mates but was glad I managed to handle the situation like I did with a huge helping of pish talk to keep him quiet.

Pot Luck

I relayed a tale in *Diary of a Taxi Driver* about Jab who always paid us five pounds, which was around double the actual fare, on condition that we take him home for nothing should he ever need it. In all the years I took him home he always had a fiver on him, so I obviously made a few pounds in tips over the years. Jab was the only person that Boss had an arrangement like this with, although there was one other regular who had a bizarre method of payment, too. His name was Billy and the first time I drove him home from the pub late one Saturday evening it went something like this. I stopped outside his house and he turned to face me. He was a big burly man, but he was friendly, just a wee bit tipsy and spoke in a brusque tone.

Billy – Do you want me to pay the fare, or take pot luck, big 'un? The choice is yours

I had no idea what the guy meant by "pot luck" so I opted to take the fare. He looked rather disappointed but handed me the exact money, shook his head slightly, and got out the car with a cheery wave back to me as he walked up his path. Cashing me in later that night, Boss went down the hire sheet making comments and observations about some of people we'd seen that particular night. He came to Billy's hire.

Boss – Oh I see you took Billy home for the first time tonight. Did he offer you "the fare or pot luck"?

Me – Aye, he did, but I had no idea what pot luck was so I went for the fare. I figured pot luck could be anything. A kiss or a cigarette or... well, anything really

Boss – Och, John. Always take pot luck if he offers it. Just sit there with both your hands held out like a bowl, and don't say a word. He'll ken you want pot luck then

Me – Err... OK

A couple of Saturdays later and Natalie shouted me over the radio to collect Billy from the Railway and take him home. He was soon in my taxi and we shortly arrived at his house, where he turned to face me.

Billy – Pot luck or the fare, big 'un?

I put my finger to my lips and looked at the roof of the car pretending to think long and hard about the choice I'd been given.

Billy (laughing) – Och come on to fuck, big 'un

I made my hands into a bowl and Billy rummaged through all the pockets in his jacket and trousers. He emptied lots of coins, a packet of chewing gum and a crumpled pack of cigarettes with about six remaining. I quickly estimated there was at least five pounds in change. My cash bag was sat on my lap with the zipped top open, so I scooted the whole lot in and retrieved the gum and cigarettes.

Billy – Looks like you did pretty well there, big 'un

Me – Thanks, Billy

Billy – Och, it's my wee game son. Occasionally there'll be fuck all, or maybe just a few pennies. Thanks for the ride home, John

I opted for pot luck every time I took Billy home and always made a healthy tip and a few battered cigarettes too. Only he and the aforementioned Jab practised these unusual payment methods. Although, there was one time when a young lad paid me in pennies bagged up in banking bags. When we ran them through Boss's coin counter later that day there were exactly three hundred of them, perfectly covering the three-pound hire. He was about sixteen years old, and it was as if he'd saved up all the pennies for a long time in order to take his first ever taxi ride.

Mathematics

Cameron, or Cammy as he liked to be called, was a lairy young man in his mid-twenties who used our taxis fairly often so I knew him quite well. He was an abrupt and direct kind of guy but he was never any bother. I remember picking him up once and he had a bottle of beer in his hand as he got in the taxi.

Me – Cammy, you shouldn't be bringing that beer bottle in here, mate

Cammy (holding the bottle up for me to see) – Look, there's only a wee bit left in it, man

Me – Well, finish it and put the empty in the door pocket, please. If Boss sees you with a bottle in here I will get his boot up my bottom

Cammy – Aye fair enough, pal

I pulled away and Cammy swigged the last remaining inch of beer, then promptly threw the bottle out the window into a field we were luckily driving past instead of a house or someone's head.

One evening he gave me a call to collect him and three of his friends from his place and take them down to Ayr. They were off for a big night out instead of confining themselves to Dalmellington. I soon picked him and his mates up, who I knew from various scenarios, and we were shortly off down the A713.

Cammy – How much is this taxi, big 'un?

Me – Twenty pounds, Cammy

Cammy (to his friends who were all in the back) – OK then boys, we need to find twenty quid for John here

They proceeded to argue and perform some of the worst mental arithmetic I'd ever heard since I was in primary school. I expected Cammy's socks to come off at one point when I saw him counting on his fingers and thought, "Well, that will get him to ten."

Cammy – Come on, lads. Four pounds each

Lad 1 – We giving John a tip then?

Lad 2 – How much is it each?

It went on and on and on. I thought that they were either mad or they were just messing about, but after many miles of this pish, I realised they just couldn't work it out. They couldn't split twenty pounds four ways.

Me – You OK there, lads?

Cammy – How much each, John?

Me – Fiver. Five pounds each, Cammy

Cammy – You sure, big 'un?

Me (glancing at him) – Aye I'm sure, Cammy. That's with no tip. If you want to throw in a tip for my mathematical help, please feel free. I did OK at maths at school. I also do a lot of these complex calculations in my line of work.

Cammy collected five pounds off each of his mates and we were sorted. Their conversation briskly switched to who will drink the most beer and have intercourse with the ugliest lady.

Tiresome Individual

The only hire I ever picked up from Coylton was a case of deliberate mathematical awkwardness, rather than the person in question just being bad at adding up. Boss sent me to pick up four people from a pub there late one weekend evening and I duly parked outside on time, walked in and found them easily enough since the pub was closing and most folks had already left. I recognised the one chap from the village, and he was with four other people all in their late thirties. I walked over to them.

Me – One of you folks booked a taxi for four people?

Mr P – Yes. Mr P is the name

Me – Aye. I'll wait for you in the car. Silver Vectra just outside

Dude – How many can you get in your taxi, pal?

Me – I can only carry four

Dude – Not five?

Me – No sorry chap. Four passengers only, I'm afraid

The others in the group looked at him as if to say "you're out of luck", and I thought no more of it. Dude wasn't nasty so I just headed on out and sat in the car knowing this was my last hire of the night and I'd soon be finished. In short order, the group of five stepped out the pub and slowly moved towards my taxi. I started the engine and sat there waiting for them to get in and assumed that the fifth person in the group would either walk off somewhere or go back in the pub. Doors opened and four people got in, with Dude leaning in through the back left door saying goodbye to his friends as I confirmed the destination with Mr P who was sat in the front seat. Nothing so far made me think that this was going to turn into an awkward and extremely irritating situation at all.

Dude – Move up there so I can get in

Dude was attempting to persuade the two ladies and the chap in the back seat to move along and let him slip in the car as well. It all seemed so hilarious as they laughed and joked, trying to squeeze along, with Dude trying desperately to lay across them and shut the door.

Dude – Bloody hell there's no room in the back of this car

I coolly looked back and broke a wee smile at the late night high jinks.

Me (chuckling) – I don't think you'll fit, Sir

His friends laughed and I shook my head as Dude squirmed and tried to cram himself into a space that wasn't there.

Dude – I don't think I'll get in

Me – OK, Sir. Let me take these good people home. You take care now

Dude's 'joke' had worn thin and I wanted to get my four passengers home and then get off home myself.

Dude – But you said you could take five passengers

Me (laughing) – Nice try, Sir, but we really need to get moving. I have to get back to Dalmellington

Dude (getting a bit cross) – You distinctly said you could carry five passengers

Now there was total silence apart from the low whine of the Vectra's engine. A quick glance at Mr P told me that Dude was getting on his nerves as well. I looked back at Dude who had backed most of the way out the car but was desperately trying to physically move one of the ladies along the back seat so he could make a bit more room for himself that would never appear. The ladies and the man in the back looked fed up too but not one of them said anything either to me or their friend who had obviously become a burden to them in the past minute or so.

Me – When did I say that?

Dude – In the pub

Me – Oh yes. I remember now. It was when I said I can only carry four passengers. You obviously heard "five" instead of "four". Easy mistake to make, Sir. No worries

Dude – You said to me...

Me (staring directly at him) – ...that I can only carry four passengers. Yes, I remember it well now, Sir. Oh, what fun we had when I said very clearly that... I... can... only... carry... four... passengers

Dude – I don't live far. I only live up the road. Can't you drop me off on the way back?

Me – Let me think about that, Sir. No. If you only live up the road you can walk. Sorry Sir, but I am not going to risk my job, however rubbish it is, to save you walking a few yards. Get out, please

The guy slowly backed out the taxi in silence, adding to the total silence from his friends which annoyed me a little bit. Not one of them told their friend to stop being such a nuisance. They may have thought he was joking like I did at first, but once they knew he seriously wanted me to take him home I half expected Mr P to say something. After Dude called me a "fanny", he slammed the car door and I slipped off the pub car park and took my four totally silent passengers home, leaving the tiresome individual with his arms outstretched in some kind of protest. None of them commented on their friend's behaviour in any way, and they didn't even try to break the incredibly tense atmosphere by talking about anything else either. I turned the radio on and listened to Radio 4 while we pootled back to Dalmellington.

Violence and Filth

Boyd's Bar sat on the main spine road through the scheme, and the only way to get from one end of Bellsbank to the other was past this hub of weekend nightlife. I would drive past it countless times every day and night, and would occasionally get a cheery wave from someone stood outside smoking a cigarette or I would witness some goings-on. Late one Friday or Saturday night, I had dropped someone off at the far end of the scheme and, after getting details of my next hire from Natalie on the radio, I headed back towards Dalmellington. As I neared Boyd's from the far side, I saw a group of about a dozen lads covering the entire width of the road outside the bar engaged in a huge punch-up. I pulled up and shouted Boss on the radio.

Me – TC6 to TC1

Boss – Go ahead, TC6

Me – I'm stuck at the far end of Bellsbank. I can't get past Boyd's. There's a huge fight going on here in the street

Boss – Fuck's sake

Me – I've got a hire from the square soon as well. Can you do it?

Boss – I can't. I'm tied up for the next ten minutes with a hire. (laughing) Run them over

Me – I can't run them over, Boss. I'll have to wait. Over and out

I sat for a minute watching the lads knocking lumps out of each other, but got bored very quickly and opted to drive ahead. I put the car in second gear and let it crawl forward with no throttle. Bracing myself for someone being thrown against the car, or at the very least a barrage of verbal abuse, I crept along. One guy even had a big stick and I hoped he didn't decide to hit the car with it. The fighting suddenly stopped and the scrapping youths parted like I was Moses and they were the Red Sea. I heard some shouting.

Youth 1 – Oh it's John. Let him through

Youth 2 – Yeah, come on lads. Get out of his way

Me (winding my window down an inch or two) – Cheers, lads

I slowly picked my speed up once I was through the melee, glanced in my mirror and slipped into third gear. The two groups of lads were once again punching and kicking viciously at each other. I shook my head and carried on with the rest of my shift which thankfully didn't require me to go back through the scheme again.

On another night, I had passed Boyd's numerous times well after it had closed its doors for that evening. The last few times I drove past there was no-one around at all, and the streets were quiet as I took babysitters and late partygoers home. It was cold and well past midnight when I drove past for the umpteenth time, and I casually noticed a male figure on Boyd's steps. Wondering what he was doing stood right outside the pub, I slowed down a wee bit. I could see a young lady with him as I drew nearer and she appeared to bend down to pick something up off the floor. Maybe she dropped her keys. Oh no, she hadn't dropped her keys! Oh, I see what's going on there now I'm almost level with them! Well, that was a bit of a surprise at that time of night in those temperatures right outside a pub.

In the four and a half years I drove the streets of the village, I can only recall one other incident of unseemly behaviour. I was sent to Burnton Club, for my first ever pick up from there, to collect someone I didn't know at all, and being new to the job they probably wouldn't know me either. I parked up outside and strolled in trying my best to look like a typical taxi driver, and soon discovered the place was a maze of rooms and was packed to the rafters. I think everyone in the area was there, which explained why the rest of the village was so quiet. I went for a wee walk round looking for my hire in a crowd of people I didn't recognise. An almost-impossible task, really.

On the few occasions I book a taxi myself, I make sure I'm either outside or just inside the door scanning everyone for the tell-tale taxi driver ID card necklace or badge. A number of the people I had to find in the early days didn't adopt this tactic, so I was left wandering around pubs and clubs like a stray dog looking for an owner.

Despite Boss giving me his usual rundown on them, which was a pretty useless "attractive lady around twenty-five years old" I had no luck spotting anyone who resembled that description. I walked into the main room of the club where the band were packing up their instruments, but the dance floor was teeming with people still eager to boogie the night away. I slipped through them to the far side of the large room, with plenty of "excuse me's" along the way as I sought my hire. Then I saw a half-naked lady who had completely removed her top and bra, asleep on her friend's shoulder. I thought I'd gone insane for a split second, and also hoped she wasn't my hire. After a good long look at her, I eventually decided she didn't fit Boss's description and headed back around the room where, fortunately, I found my attractive lady at the bar and we soon departed.

Vomit

Vomit, spew or pavement pizza (as it is sometimes hilariously referred to) is a hazard for anyone, not just taxi drivers. I managed to totally avoid such an occurrence in my cab over the years and only had the one very close shave mentioned in my first book. While that was a close call, and this next incident was not as close, it could have been far worse.

Tony was a guy in his late twenties I picked up very rarely, to be honest, but I liked him, and on the few hires I did take him home we always had a nice chat about fairly interesting topics which made a nice change from the drunken pish talk I had to endure with most other folks. He had a fairly interesting job, which I liked to hear about, and he was the same about my taxi driving, I think. Boss called me over the radio to pick Tony up from the Black Bull as I returned back to the village from an outside hire one busy weekend evening.

I duly pulled up outside and spotted him immediately. He was sensibly waiting for me just outside the pub door and was soon in the back seat of my cab. He was also one of the very few people who took the back seat in all the years I did the job. A few other folk were on the pavement chatting and saying goodbye to each other as the night drew to a close.

Me – Hi Tony

Tony – Hi John

Me – Home, Tony?

Tony – Aye, pal, but we just need to wait for my brother. He'll be along in a minute

Me – OK, no worries

I didn't have a pressing need to speed things along so I sat and gazed idly out the car windscreen while we chatted about nothing in particular. A guy who had been leaning against the pub wall for a while suddenly started retching and spewing profusely. I have never seen so much vomit come out of one person in my life. I thought he would faint or pass out it was so violent, and people moved well out of his way in utter disgust as he held onto a drainpipe and jettisoned sick in a huge arc away from himself.

Me – Bloody hell, Tony. Look at that poor guy over there. I have never seen that much spew in my life. Glad he isn't in this car

Tony – The bad news is, John, that guy is my brother, Rob

Me – Oh. I hope he's OK

Tony – Och, he'll be fine once he's finished. He's done this many times

Me – Jeez. OK you're the boss, Tony

Normally, there was no way I would entertain letting a guy in that state get in the car, but he'd managed to aim everything away from himself and after a moment or so to regain his composure he looked fine. He ambled over to the car, opened the door, got in and sat down.

Rob – Sorry about that

Me – I was a bit worried you'd disappear with all that coming out of you

Rob – Aye, it looks awful but I'm fine now, pal

It was as if he'd never been sick in his life. He looked absolutely fine, and the brief journey back to Tony's passed without a repeat performance.

Poor Decisions

We now turn our attention to a family that I got to know very well over the course of my taxi-driving tenure. Joan and Ron and their daughter Kate. One particular weekday, Kate phoned me up about noon and I answered on my earpiece because I had just set off on a hire. She was a smart lass in her early twenties who lived near Ayr after moving out the family home shortly after I started the job.

Me – Hello, T&C Taxis

Kate – Hi, John. It's Kate. Could you bring my father over today?

Me – Aye, but I can't see to him for an hour I'm afraid. I'm just off to Ayr with a hire now

Kate – Oh that's fine, John. Whenever really

Me – OK then. I'll get your dad about 1pm

Kate – Great. I'll tell him

After memorising that I need to pick Ron up at 1pm (I would

write it on the booking sheet once I dropped my current hire off in Ayr), I pootled off to Ayr with my regular noon hire. I didn't even get out of Dalmellington when the phone rang again.

Me – Hello, T&C Taxis

Kate – Hi John. It's me again

Me – Hi Kate

Kate – Can you cancel my father's taxi, please? Sorry

Me – Aye no worries. Thanks for letting me know

I continued on my way to Ayr, then drove back and returned to Dalmellington about 1pm, pulled up outside the taxi office and the phone rang once more.

Me – Hello, T&C Taxis

Kate – Hi, John. It's Kate again. Sorry about this but could you come over here and pick something up for my father?

Inwardly, I rolled my eyes and thought of the wasted journey I'd just undertaken back from Ayr. However, the A713 is a nice road to drive along, although I would much prefer to be on a motorcycle than a dull four-door saloon, and I knew I would soon make another two trips down it that day.

Me – I can. What am I picking up? Is it big and bulky?

Kate – No. It's an envelope

Me – OK. I'll be there in thirty minutes

Kate – Great

Now if she'd have phoned me earlier, I could have dropped off my hire in Ayr at about half past twelve not that far from where Kate lived and got to her much sooner. I did mention I was heading to Ayr when she phoned but I guess that slipped her mind. Due to me having nothing else on for the next hour, I had a few drags on a cigarette and a swig or two of microwaved coffee before heading off once more for the lovely seaside town of Ayr, and soon reached Kate's house. She gave me a wee brown envelope and told me it had some money in it for her father, which was information I didn't need to know, and she also paid the taxi fare.

I tried to treat such package carrying exercises like a *Transporter* movie where Jason Statham would carry anything for anyone to anywhere, without knowing what was in the package. I drove back to Dalmellington and delivered it to Ron. Thinking back to earlier, Kate wanted me to pick her father up, take him to her house, then most likely bring him back just to get the envelope. It would have cost her twice as much because I'd be carrying her father two ways. I guess she must have thought of that, which is why she cancelled the original hire, but it was a pity she didn't think to phone for the second hire earlier.

Here's another brief example of her wasteful use of money. I got into work one particular Monday morning, and Boss was laughing and shaking his head as soon as I walked in through the office door. He usually greeted me with a cheerful grunt or a "good morning, you Brummie bastard", so I knew something hilarious had happened since I left on Saturday afternoon.

Me – Morning, Boss

Boss (chuckling) – Morning, John. Oh, I had a good hire on Saturday evening to Kate's

Me – Ron and Joan popping over for a cup of tea, were they? Nice chat on the drive over?

Boss (laughing more now) – Even more bizarre. Kate phoned and wanted me to take a packet of tobacco over!

Me – For fuck's sake!

Boss – Aye. A twenty-odd pound hire to deliver a wee pouch of tobacco. Unbelievable

Me – Words actually fail me, Boss. There's a corner shop a few hundred yards from her house

Boss – Ours is not to reason why, John

A true enough statement, but it always baffled me how people as bright as Kate was, and she was a smart young woman, made decisions like that. The money that she and other people threw away was astonishing.

Boss's Beloved Mug and the Office Tidy Up

The taxi office was a bit of a mess some of the time. It was actually a lot of a mess most of the time. OK, it was a total mess all of the time. A teenager's bedroom merged with a council tip and a scrapyard would come close to describing it. Actually, that's a bit unfair on tips and scrap yards, which are some of the neatest workspaces I have seen. When I first started the job, it wasn't too bad though. A half-decent sofa that I could stretch out on during quiet periods. A wooden chair which the senior ladies would prefer to the pair of unmatched, saggy and hard to get out of armchairs. A portable gas bottle fuelled heater. Boss's ancient computer complete with a sea of paperwork that defied belief in its complexity and untidiness. The kitchen area had a fridge which only ever had a bottle of milk in it, a microwave dubbed Old Sparky and whichever was the latest cheap kettle being sold in the village pound shop. That was about it, really, except for one sacred item which Boss explained to me on the day I started: his tea mug.

We all, or at least many of us, have a favourite drinking vessel. It may sport a design we like, our favourite football team or a witty phrase. Boss's mug was a fairly generic one which was very old and bore the design of a shire horse. He explained that a much-loved relative bought it him many years ago and that if I ever broke it, he would sharply jam his boot up my Brummie bottom. I got the picture very quickly and I henceforth handled Boss's mug like it was a Ming vase. It was cracked and stained and chipped, and seemed to be held together by magic rather than any structural integrity. It looked flimsy and about to break at any moment, and I feared that one day it would shatter into its component atoms which meant I hoped that someone, or Boss himself, would break the damn thing rather than myself be the perpetrator of 'mugicide'. My own mugs were pound shop or village charity shop items that I would pick up for fifty pence or less, and I would replace them every month or so when they got too filthy. I was too lazy to wash them and the sink in the taxi office wasn't much better than the state my mug got into anyway.

The years rolled by and Boss's mug ploughed on relentlessly. It saw off every attempt at breaking it that Boss or anyone else could devise. The shire horse motif faded as time passed and the glaze deteriorated. Every time I handed it to Boss when I made him a drink was met with him remarking how much he loved the mug, and how much peril anyone who broke it was in. Consequently, I took the care of his mug very seriously. Making Boss a cup of tea one day like I'd done many times over the years, the bottom cracked and tea spewed from it. Milliseconds later, the side of the mug became totally detached and fell noisily to the floor in a shower of tea and shards of faded shire horse. Boss shouted from the wee office.

Boss – What's that I hear, Lockett?

Me – Your sacred tea mug has broken

I expected a stream of foul language as Boss ambled into the kitchen area and gazed down at me picking up the larger of the broken bits of mug. He removed his specs and placed them on his balding head as I stood up and held out shards of crockery.

Me – Got any Sellotape, Boss?

Boss (laughing) – Och to fuck. I don't really give a shit about the stupid mug anyway, you Brummie idiot

Me – Boss, you old bastard. I actually thought you did care about it

We laughed like drains. He paid a quick visit to the pound shop and returned proudly brandishing a mug which bore a generic design of a wee dog. I made him a tea in it and handed it over.

Boss – Now then, Lockett. This mug with the cute wee doggie on it has been in my family for about twenty years and I treasure it very much. If anything happens to it I will beat you to a pulp with that tyre lever over there

Me – Boss, I have to inform you that my Phineas and Ferb mug has been in my family since the late eighteenth century, so bollocks to you

I don't think two cabbies have ever laughed so much, although for a split second I thought he was serious. He was that good at kidding on.

Over the years, detritus in the office accumulated and would never leave. Boss seemed to have a phobia about disposing of junk, or at least moving it somewhere more suitable. The cellar would have been an ideal location for all the old car wheels and various bits of car trim and parts that gravitated inwards. It wasn't a true cellar through a trapdoor or anything, rather a room way off down the end of a long corridor that had about four steps down to it through a low doorway. It was dark, dreary and dank.

Like a black hole swallowing a star, our taxi office took everything in. There were two bouncy castles and their inflating fans that we could never fold up correctly so they always took up more space than necessary. Boss hired them out very occasionally for local parties and events. I found a workshop repair manual for a weird type of Hyundai that Boss explained to me he had owned many years previously. A broken jet washer, jumper cables, tools and undelivered books lay in haphazard piles here and there.

Books took up most of the cellar too and had turned mouldy with time. The entire dome of bricks, which formed the Frankenstein's laboratory-like cellar, reeked of damp books and was quite painful to the nose. The often-blocked toilet just next to the cellar door didn't help the awful aroma either. The book clubs and catalogue companies responsible for the numerous undelivered paperbacks were very poor at arranging their collection from us. Customers would refuse them at the door, Bruce the regular parcel guy or myself would bring them back and Boss would inform the supplier. They never got picked up and we never got asked to send them on anywhere else either. A total waste of what may have been perfectly good reads for some people sat in our stinking cellar to rot for years. Boss, being a bit of a stickler for rules and regulations, didn't like to throw them away or even take them to the charity shop before they turned mouldy in case the supplier did suddenly ask for them to be returned, but this never happened.

In any case, what this ridiculous state of affairs meant

was that the one place we could have stored car parts and the bouncy castles and all the other junk taking up floor space in the waiting area was full of mouldy stinking books. 99 per cent of our customers would phone for a cab, or if they walked to our office, we would take them as soon as they came through the door, but in rare instances, some would need a seat for a few moments. Our crowded waiting area and cluttered chairs meant they would sit on a chair arm or stand amid a sea of detritus. Seemingly unaware or reluctant to see what a dump the office was, Boss actually forbid any of us to tidy it up. I hated the mess, but seeing as I spent most of my time driving I didn't lose much sleep over it.

What made the situation even more frustrating, if that was even possible, was Boss's own untidiness. I remember one quiet lunchtime when I was feasting on a soup and roll while Boss munched on a ham sandwich. I sat atop three car tyres conveniently plonked on the office floor while Boss perched himself on the sole remaining seat which was right next to the portable gas bottle heater. The office was at 'peak mess' at this point in time, and we almost had to take turns in moving around the cramped and cluttered floorspace. Screwing his face up in disgust, Boss pulled a strip of fat off the edge of a piece of ham poking from his sandwich and dropped it on top of the hot heater top where it slowly sizzled. I stared at the nearby pedal bin, an amazing item in the office to be honest, made a remark to Boss about the totally unnecessary mess he had just made and shook my head. He announced it was his office so he could do what he liked, which, although technically correct, wasn't the answer I was expecting.

In sharp contrast, Boss was quite rightly very fussy about

the cleanliness of the taxis, and despite my own car being an utter mess with the carpet thick in cigarette ash and sweet wrappers, I kept my taxi very clean indeed. Part of my Sunday daily routine was to clean my taxi thoroughly, and even though I say so myself, I think I did a pretty good job. The car that Boss tended to drive was a Vectra estate car, mine being a saloon, and he used his car like an office. With letters wedged in the windscreen and dashboard joint, the door pockets full of sweeties and the boot always full of junk whenever I had to use it, his taxi was a bit messy to say the least. One day, for reasons I never quite discovered, he announced he was going to inspect my taxi and we stepped outside. I lit up a cigarette while he went over every inch of the car with a fine-toothed comb, tutting and mumbling to himself. Finally, he opened the boot and beckoned me over with his glasses perched on top of his head and a mean glint in his eye. There was never anything in the boot of my taxi, so I ambled over wondering to myself what could possibly be wrong.

Boss – Lockett, this car is an absolute disgrace. What is that doing in your boot?

I peered into the totally empty boot and shrugged my shoulders.

Me – What mess? There's nothing in there, man

Boss (pointing vigorously) – That, there!

I noticed the very end of a white piece of cloth poking out from underneath the boot floor liner and I quickly realised it was the rag I used to wipe the dipstick when I did my daily oil level check. I used to lift the floor up and toss the rag into the space where the spare wheel, jack and tools sat, then drop the floor down. On this occasion, a corner of rag the size of a matchbox was now visible.

Me (rolling my eyes) – Jeez!

I lifted the floor, moved the rag, and dropped the floor back down again.

Me – Now, let us make our way over to your car, shall we? The mobile council tip

Boss – You cheeky sod!

Boss's vehicle fleet varied over the years in number and size and type of vehicle depending on the taxi, parcels and bouncy castle situation. During the early years, I drove a silver Vauxhall Vectra B until Boss replaced it with a silver Vectra C, which I then used despite it being his newest vehicle. He also owned two other Vectras, one of which was a claret-coloured type B estate he used mostly, a Citroen minibus, a Ford Escort van and a Transit van. All of these vehicles were diesel powered and filling a vehicle with petrol never happened because Boss didn't have any petrol-powered cars, so the opportunity never reared its ugly head.

Then Boss bought a Nissan Primera saloon with a petrol engine to replace one of the Vectras that had passed the local council's age limit for taxis, which I believe was eight years. I drove it a few times, when mine was being serviced or whatever, and didn't like it much. I didn't really like driving the Vectra or indeed any car at all to be perfectly frank, but it seemed a better car for cabbing in than the Primera did in my opinion and the Vauxhall had a better heater, which was very important. Thankfully, Boss drove it for the most part, and eventually, he refuelled one of the diesel cars with petrol, having got used to refuelling the Primera with it.

Over the next few weeks, his misfuelling of various cars became a regular occurrence and it reached the farcical point when he misfuelled twice in one day. I avoided Boss as much as possible that day until I could cash in and go home. The next morning, I walked into the office around 8am. Bruce the parcel guy and Geoff, who did a long and complicated school run in the minibus, were already there. Boss sat behind the Perspex screen to the wee office and repositioned his spectacles onto the top of his head as soon as I walked in.

Me – Morning, everyone

Bruce – Morning, John

Geoff – Morning, big 'un

Boss – Right then. Now you're here, John, I can give you all this lecture I've been stewing on since yesterday. Misfuelling vehicles. It has to stop. You all need to take better notice of what fuel the vehicle you're filling up needs. We've had far too many...

Geoff – Err... Hold your horses there, Boss. I've never misfuelled a vehicle in my life

Boss – I'm not naming any one individual, Geoff. I'm just making a general point about the careless approach that...

Geoff – Have you ever misfuelled, John?

Me – No, I haven't

Geoff – Have you, Bruce?

Bruce – No. I'm glad to say I haven't either

Geoff – There you go, Boss. The only bloke you need to have a word with is yourself

Boss (apoplectic) – It doesn't fuckin' matter *who* did the misfuelling, Geoff! We *all* need to be wary of doing it!

Geoff – No, we don't. *You* need to be more wary of doing it. Not us

Boss and Geoff proceeded to have a top level and very loud argument so I quietly grabbed my taxi keys, then slipped back outside and checked my cab over. A few minutes later, Boss emerged from the office, mumbled to me that I was doing my usual runs that particular morning, and drove off to begin his school-kid runs. Then Geoff stepped outside followed by Bruce and we all silently started our working day. That day got considerably worse when Boss unbelievably misfuelled yet again.

A few weeks later, Boss and myself were stood outside the office watching the world go by and talking about nothing of importance when one of Andy's taxis drove past. I noticed a big sticker over the fuel cap which read 'Diesel'.

Me – That's a good idea, Boss

Boss – What's that?

Me – Andy's cab just went by and I saw a sticker over the fuel cap saying 'diesel'. Good idea, I think. You should put stickers like that on all your vehicles

Boss – Nah. Stupid idea

I thought it was a no-brainer but what did I know. Fortunately, Boss sold the Nissan after a few months and he never owned another petrol-engined vehicle.

Returning to the issue of mess and junk in the office, I wearily strolled in to start another day of cabbing one particular day. Boss waved a piece of paper at me that looked like a letter.

Boss – Ah morning, John

Me – Morning, Boss. What's that you're waving at me? Some pish I bet

Boss – Aye, it's pish all right. The council are coming to inspect the office to ascertain its suitability as a taxi office. All taxi offices in the area have to be approved, much like cars and drivers. We have to get this place tidied up, laddie

Me – Jeez. Do you know a guy with a bulldozer?

Boss – You cheeky cunt, Lockett. We'll have this place right enough in no time

Me – Really? What's the plan?

Boss – We have plenty of time. One day next week when the wee 'uns are off school, Geoff will get the big Transit van and we'll dump everything in there. Natalie will spruce the place up after that

Me – Decent enough plan, I suppose

The following week when the kids were off school, Geoff showed up on one of his days off and the Big Office Tidy Up leapt into action. I say 'leapt'; more like crawled and stuttered. The Transit van was coaxed into life and was backed up to the office door. Boss left me with the phone and I left him and Geoff to what would be a tiring few hours of de-cluttering the office. I'm glad that Boss didn't opt to drive himself and leave me to tidy up. Cleaning up someone else's avoidable mess is something I would rather not do. Every so often I would park up outside the office and poke my head round the corner to see the progress, note that not much had been done, and promptly get back in my taxi and slope off to the Pit Stop snack bar behind the village filling station.

After much longer than the tidy up should have taken, Boss shouted me over the radio that the office was now in "immaculate" condition and that I should come for a look. I swiftly returned and walked inside to be met by a sight I thought I'd never see. The carpet was now visible and chairs could be sat on. The sofa was free of bouncy castles and sundry other junk. No tools and car parts were strewn around the place. There was even a silly wee plastic flower in a vase hastily obtained from the charity shop. Natalie busied herself vacuuming and giving the whole place a damn good clean which the office hadn't seen in years.

Me – When is the inspection by the council?

Boss – A few weeks' time. I want this office keeping clean as well. No mess whatsoever. It stays like this

Me – Suits me, Boss

Natalie – Suits me too. I don't ever want this place as bad again

In those few weeks, I got used to working from a neat and tidy office and it was nice to be able to stretch out on the sofa once again. The few customers who actually came to the office were amazed by the new surroundings and it became a bit of a talking point around the village.

A few weeks later, a council official duly arrived to inspect the premises and I returned from a hire just as they were leaving. Boss stood outside with a big cheesy grin on his face holding the piece of council approved paperwork certifying our office as suitable. I sparked up a cigarette as Boss explained the boring details to me. I nodded and voiced my total disinterest with the minute details he insisted on relaying to me, but I was sharply brought back to reality with Boss's next sentence once he'd finished his lecture.

Boss – I'll go and get the Transit from Alan's and we'll empty everything back into the office

Me – What?! You're going to put everything back in there? The bouncy castles? The car parts? All that bloody junk?

Boss – It's not "junk", as you put it

Me – Most of it is. Anyway, can't we clear that cellar out and put everything down there? Those books are no use to anyone. Make more sense than turning the office into a tip again

Boss – We can't dump the books and I'm not having my bouncy castles in that damp environment. I'll go and get the Transit

Boss trundled off to retrieve the Transit van full of junk back from his friend Alan's place while I took a last fond look around the office. I had a quick lie down on the sofa and inwardly shook my head at the sheer insanity of what would soon happen. Boss returned and we unloaded all the rubbish back into our once presentable office. Admittedly it was much tidier than before the whole exercise began weeks before, but all the same, it seemed like madness to me. Over the course of the next few weeks, it was back to how it always had been: a teenager's bedroom mixed with a council tip and a scrapyard.

Restraining Order

Chaz was quite a character around the village who often got into scrapes, drunk a wee bit too much from time to time and had numerous encounters with local law enforcement. Trivial encounters to be fair, but he just seemed to be one of those lads who couldn't escape the routine his life had sadly become. I liked the guy to be honest, and often cringed at his latest escapades whenever I took him home. I was at the Pit Stop gaining some urgently needed energy from one of their supreme sausage sandwiches one mundane weekday when Boss phoned me.

Boss – Chaz wants a taxi home. He's in the square now

Me – Roger

I arrived in the square a few minutes later; Chaz bounded over and was in my taxi in seconds.

Me – Hi, Chaz

Chaz – Morning, John. Hang on a bit. My mother is just coming out the Spar

Me – How are things with you, Chaz?

Chaz – Meh. Police bothering me. Fuckin' council going on to me about the usual pish

Me – Yeah. Bloody council

Always agree with the punter. A rule I established very early on in the job. We waited a minute or two which gave me enough time to polish off the sandwich I'd nestled in my lap, then his mother appeared and got in the back. She was a lady I had taken home a few times over the years, and on one occasion had to physically haul her up a flight of stairs to her flat due to her very intoxicated state.

Me – Hello, Mrs C

Mrs C – Hi, John

Me – Home, Chaz? Or somewhere else?

Chaz – Home please, John

Mrs C – No... We need to go and get some coal from the filling station

Chaz – Fuck the coal. We're going home, Mother

Mrs C – But we need coal, Son

Chaz – If we go down the filling station, there's more chance the police will spot me, and I'm in a bad situation here. They'll be at the Pit Stop round about now scoffing and drinking tea. We're going home

I drove on and headed for Chaz's place, but being the inquisitive guy I am, I just had to ask why he was so keen to avoid the police in this "bad situation" as he put it. The situation of being in a taxi was not the sort of offence that Strathclyde Police were known to be clamping down on. Uncannily, there was a police car at the filling station when I left minutes earlier.

Me – So, Chaz. What have you been up to then?

Chaz – Oh just the fuckin' usual drugs and stuff. The police will lift me if they see me with my mother because I'm not allowed to talk to her or even be with her due to a restraining order

Me – Oh

Chaz was not allowed to talk to, or even *be* with his own mother, which I thought was a peculiar and terrible state to be in, and I did wonder how he even got into such a position in the first place.

Mr Bagoo

One senior gentleman I took from the office to his sister's house every Sunday I named Mr Bagoo. He was a very nice guy who would get the 52 bus from Ayr, then use a taxi for the last mile or so to her place in Burnton. He spoke in a very slow and low hushed tone, which I always struggled to hear, and was the most unobservant and clumsy man I have ever met who never seemed to notice anything that went on around him. He always had very bulky shopping bags with him too, which he draped over the gear stick, and would apologise profusely while taking what seemed like forever to untangle them so I could drive off. Whenever he paid me, it would always be in fiddly coins where he would get the denominations mixed up before dropping them all over the car. His bulky awkward bags together with his unobservant nature and clumsiness, like the television cartoon character Mr Magoo, led to my nickname for him.

He'd lived in Burnton himself many years previously and worked at the nearby coal mine, so I always assumed he knew the area quite well, but this turned out not to be true at all. After he'd finally removed his bags from the gear stick we were on our way, and I was soon heading past Sillyhole Farm towards the wee community of Burnton.

Mr B (looking to his left past Sillyhole) – Ooh there's a lorry over there. When did they build a road behind Sillyhole?

Me – I don't think there is a road there, unless they quickly laid one overnight

Mr B – Well there's a lorry in that field. How did that get there then?

I took a wee glance over to where he was pointing.

Me – That's a tractor in a field, Sir

Mr B – Oh…

Parcel Delivery Man

Wrong Number

Delivering parcels in part of a town I didn't know very well meant I usually took longer than normal. When you also consider the number of streets that are poorly numbered and illogically laid out everything took longer still. The overwhelming majority of roads are laid out quite sensibly, however, with numbers actually following in numerical order, which helped. Looking for number 39 in Soandso Road seemed like another easy task. I passed number 23 on the left side meaning that number 25 would be next after the left-hand curve that the road suddenly took. I glanced at the next house on the left as the road straightened out again and noticed a big shiny number 39 on it, not number 25 as I was expecting. I quickly assumed that the break in numbers must have been made for some reason, so I parked up at the bottom of the short driveway. Not noticing any numbered dustbins to confirm anything else, I was soon knocking at the door. A lady answered.

Me – Hello, Madam. I've got a parcel for a Mrs Morrison

Lady – Oh that's not me. She lives at number 39, just up the street

Me (looking quite intently at the large and shiny 39 on the door) – Oh. I thought this was number 39

Lady – No. This is number 25

Me – Oh. This is Soandso Road, though?

Lady – Yes

Me (laughing) – Oh well at least I got that right. I was confused by the large, shiny and actually very nice number 39 you have on your door there

I pointed at the very noticeable number and the lady turned round and followed my finger.

Lady – Oh, yes. This front door is from Mrs Morrison's house. They had a new front door and I had their old one. My old door was terrible

We did have a wee chuckle over the incident and I soon delivered to the correct house, which also had a nice and shiny number 39 emblazoned on it. I wished every house had such brilliant shiny numbers, but only on the appropriate house, and I never noticed if the lady at number 25 ever changed the number, but once again it was a detail burned hard into my head map.

No-one Here By That Name
Like many communities around the country, one of my rare parcel rounds was in a part of town where the houses were numbered by someone with either a cruel sense of humour or an issue with numbers being in... well... numerical order... any order. I wouldn't have minded if the houses had been in

alphabetical order. Eight, five, four, nine, one, seven, six, ten, three and two would have been better than the utter chaos of this particular part of town. Adding to the proceedings were the too-often-seen poorly numbered house or the house with no number at all. I was always glad to see dustbins, or 'buckets' as they were termed, sat outside various abodes, as many of them were adorned with huge numbers, which gave me clues as to where a certain house may be.

My procedure for delivering in this maze of numeric dyslexia was to park the taxi outside the local shop, which was fairly central, and have a leisurely stroll with the handful of parcels tucked under an arm. My memory worked overtime in an attempt to remember which house was where in readiness for the next time. I walked up to number 127 guided by the bucket outside and knocked the door. A young lad about eighteen years old answered.

Me – Hello, Sir. I have a parcel here for a Mrs Collins

Lad – No-one here by that name, pal

A quick glance at the large green bucket confirmed a huge number 127 and the front door had a large and very legible 127 on it also.

Me – Sorry about that, Sir. I guess I must have some old or incorrect information here

I turned and stepped away a few paces as I headed for the next house on my route.

Lad – They'll be back later

Me (turning around) – Pardon, Sir? "They'll be back later?" You said there was "no-one here by that name"

Lad – There isn't anyone here by that name

Me – Oh… right… sorry, Sir, I got mixed up there. I thought for one minute you said they would be back later

Lad – Yeah, they will be back later

Now, this was a first. Not only that, it was quite probably the most ridiculous way to say that a certain person wasn't at home but would be back later. Was he being deliberately awkward? Or just couldn't phrase himself better? I stood right back on his doorstep.

Me – Sorry about this, Sir, but I seem to be misunderstanding you. I blame my Birmingham ears. Is there a Mrs Collins here?

Lad – No

Me – OK then. Does a Mrs Collins live here at all, and they are out at this precise moment?

Lad – Yes, she's out

Me – So. In conclusion, then. There is a Mrs Collins at this address, but just not physically here at this moment in time.

Maybe at work, or the local shop or a relative's house or on holiday in Uruguay?

Lad – She's just nipped out to her friend's house up the street

Me – Oh I see. Well, in that case, could you take this parcel on their behalf? That would be great and I'm sure Mrs Collins would appreciate it very much

Lad – Aye. Sure, pal

The lad took the parcel and signed my gadget. Should I explain where I think he went wrong? Err… yeah.

Me – My name is John and I pride myself on doing the best I can at this job. Delivering parcels for people. You know what I mean? I like to get it right. You understand me?

Lad – Aye. I understand you, pal

Me – Good. I'm glad to hear that because we very nearly managed a 'failure to deliver' situation here. Do you have any idea how that nearly happened?

Lad – No

The lad looked serious. I don't think he had a single shred of a clue as to why I nearly took the parcel away, with the reason for non-delivery being "person no longer at this address".

Me – Oh. The very first sentence you spoke after I said I had a parcel for Mrs Collins was, and correct me if I'm wrong, was something along the lines of "No-one here by that name," which implies... infers... whatever... that there is no Mrs Collins living, resident, inhabiting here at all. Do you understand how I may think from your response of "no-one here by that name" that there is no Mrs Collins here at all?

Lad – You've lost me, pal

Me – Aha! In that case, Sir, I bid you good day and sorry if I have caused you any inconvenience

Lad – Aye. See you, pal

I honestly think that I would have simply wasted my effort trying to explain what I meant any further, and opted to not let the conversation descend into a Monty Python type sketch, so I left it at that. I burned 127 Soandso Street and Mrs Collins into my memory and pressed on with the remainder of my parcels.

I'll Get My Dad

On my parcel round in Ayr one day, I was bearing a package for number 15, which meant I was looking for the eighth house on the left along this particular road. Most streets work like this but there are always exceptions to this common-sense rule even if a lot of local councils seem to lack any. I spotted number 13, then another street split off to the left, then the next two houses didn't have numbers on, but being the shrewd delivery man I now thought I was meant that I opted for the first house after the junction. However, like I said, you never know, so I always asked, especially if they haven't got a number anywhere and I liked to make my point. A young girl about eighteen years old answered the door.

Me – Is this number 15?

Her – I'll get my dad

Me – Is this number 15?

Her – I'll get my dad

Me – Only get him if this is number 15. I don't want to waste his time

Her – I'll get my dad

Me (giving up) – OK the parcel is for a Mr Soandso

Her – MUM!!!

Mum arrived and business was concluded fairly quickly after I made my point about the house not having a number on it. I did wonder why the daughter couldn't answer a question like "Is this number 15?" and also, why keep saying "I'll get my dad" if he's not in and you shout for your mum?

Dogs

Delivery guys and gals have a reputation for encountering problems with dogs. Postworkers are renowned for being bitten by them, but I never had any problems at all. I think the dogs I encountered were more trouble for their owners than for delivery people. I arrived at number 9 in a street I had been down many times, but I'd never noticed the house before. It was just like any other house along the street, and even though I had delivered a number of parcels to Mrs F at number 10 directly opposite, nothing had ever caused me to even glance over at number 9. That was until I eventually had a parcel for the place, but since I had a parcel for number 10 as well, I parked up outside Mrs F's and walked over. The front garden was strewn with rubbish and the large lounge window had a huge broken pane in it with polythene film covering the gaping hole. I braced myself and strode up the short pathway.

I knocked the door and could instantly hear the sound of two yapping dogs from inside. They arrived at the door in seconds, but I could tell from their barking that they were wee Yorkshire Terriers or something similar, and not being afraid of dogs I gave the matter no thought whatsoever. Through the heavily patterned glass, I saw an enormous man slowly waddle towards the door and I just held out the parcel in anticipation.

As soon as the door opened, the two wee dogs zoomed out like bullets and were off down the street. They were so quick I couldn't even confirm their breed.

Mr Smith – Shit!!

Me – Parcel for Mr Smith

Mr Smith – Aye

He took the parcel and I offered him the gadget. He shakily signed it and passed it back to me peering around the road.

Me – Thank you, Sir

Mr Smith – Can you see my dogs, pal?

Me (glancing round) – No I can't. Sorry

Mr Smith – Shit! This happens every time I open the bloody door

Me – Oh... Err... Bye, Sir

I left him to what would probably be a long and tiring search for his dogs and stepped over the road to drop off Mrs F's parcel. I knocked her door, then watched Mr Smith wobble around his front garden kicking bits of junk about as he shouted for his dogs to return. Mrs F opened her door and watched him with me for a while.

Mrs F – What is that man doing?

Me (turning round) – Oh hi, Mrs F. His dogs have run off

Mrs F – I think I would too

Further round the scheme I had a very regular parcel drop

off at number 42. The first time I went there, the lady of the house darted out from round the back like a rocket and met me halfway up the garden path before I got anywhere near the door. She gave me a very animated "shh" routine with her finger to her lips and led me back down to the roadside. We had a brief chat in barely audible whispers.

Lady – Och you'll have to be very quiet. My husband is asleep. He works night shifts and hates being woken up

Me – Aye that's no problem. My dad worked night shifts when I was a boy so I know how difficult it can be

Lady – There's a wee porch round the back. If I'm not here, just pop any parcels in there. It's never locked, but please be very quiet

Me – OK, Madam, that's fine by me

The lady took the parcel and that was that. The next time I had a delivery for the same house I remembered about the guy working nights so I crept round the back, easily opened the wee porch door and gently placed the parcel on a nearby stool. It made no noise whatsoever, except the inaudible sound of parcel molecules touching stool molecules at very low velocity, but the dog in the house heard it and barked its head off. It was a big, loud dog too. I cringed, closed the door and quickly got back to my taxi and could still hear the dog even after I'd started the car back up. It was louder than a Motorhead concert, which did beg the question... If you work nights and want the delivery guy to be very quiet, which I was, why have you got a very loud dog which barks its head off at the slightest noise? Every time I delivered there was the same story, and even knowing that the dog would bark its incredibly loud head off, I still crept around the place afraid to make even the slightest noise myself. I saw the lady of the house once again when she met me halfway down the path and the dog was going absolutely bonkers in the house. It was breaking all sorts of noise records and I did mention it, but I don't think she saw my point at all.

The Test

Boss (over the radio) – TC1 to TC6

Me – Go ahead, TC1

I was heading back to the office after a hire on an average Sunday afternoon. Boss was out and about in his taxi somewhere in the village.

Boss – Go to Boyd's Bar and pick up Mr M and take him home. He's half asleep and blootered, apparently. Oh, and he can be a bit tiresome. I'd do the hire myself for reasons that may become apparent to you, but I need to see Mr Brown now, and Mr M wants a taxi sharpish

Me – Roger

I wondered what Boss meant by "reasons that may become apparent". I assumed that Mr M could be a bit of a live wire but wasn't too concerned. I had been doing the job for a few years by now, and nothing much really bothered me. Boss gave me some directions to Mr M's abode, which was a very remote farmhouse I'd never been to before, although I had been down a nearby lane on the back road to Cumnock a few times. Even though I had no satnav device, I knew I would find the place easily enough, even if Mr M was asleep the entire journey.

I found Mr M snoring loudly in one of Boyd's comfy armchairs, and together with a couple of his friends we had him in my taxi and were soon on our way. The miles passed agreeably enough with Mr M spending the vast majority of the journey dozing off and myself wondering how asleep he'd be by the time we got to his house. I decided to turn the radio on and deliberately hit a few potholes to try to keep Mr M awake but it didn't work. He eventually woke up at a very opportune moment just before I arrived at the end of his gated driveway which led up to his impressive house. He gestured me to pull in as he reached into a pocket to retrieve his wallet.

Mr M – How much do I owe you, big 'un?

I told him the fare and he peeled off some notes. I already had the change ready in my hand, but he waved it away. He folded his wallet and stuffed it back in his jacket pocket then exited the car easily enough followed by a cheery wave. I made sure he looked steady enough on his feet before pulling away thinking what a nice guy he was. He was no bother at all and I made a welcome few pounds for a tip. Obviously Boss and Mr M have had a problem or two in the past I surmised, which is probably why I was given advanced warning of his nature, but that turned out to be unnecessary.

After a mile or so I reached down to turn up the volume on the CD player as I headed back to Dalmellington, and noticed three twenty-pound notes lying in the passenger footwell on the left side by the door. "Oh dear," I thought. Sixty pounds is a lot of money and I was a bit short of cash at the time, but after thinking for a split second about keeping it, I left them where they were until I got back to base. I shouted Boss on the radio once I was back in the village and he gave me the all clear, so I headed back to the office.

Holding the three notes in my hand, I ambled in the taxi waiting room and Boss peered at me over his reading glasses from behind the Perspex screen to the wee office.

Boss – Was Mr M any bother?

Me – No. He was asleep for most of the time and he even gave me a wee tip

Boss – Och well that's OK then. He can be a bit of a problem sometimes, in case you get him again

Me – Well there is one, what you might call "problem"

Boss – What's that?

Me – He dropped this

By now I had walked around the wee partition to the office and I held out the sixty pounds. Boss laughed.

Boss – Och deary me. He's a crafty one that Mr M

Me – Sorry Boss, I don't see what is so "crafty" about losing sixty quid

Boss – Och John it's a test. The guy doesn't ken who you are and if he can trust you. He dropped the sixty quid to test your trustworthiness

Me – Sorry Boss but I must be Johnny McThicko. Why is he testing me? I'm a licenced PHV driver. I've passed background checks. I took him home safely. Nothing else to worry about

Boss (touching his nose with his finger) – Aha!

Me – Is he a spy or something? Jimmy McBond, och och seven?

Boss – Och no, John. In a week or so, or maybe longer, Mr M will need your services to do a wee job for him. Nothing illegal. I ken you Brummies frown on doing illegal things. It will be a job that will require your discretion and honesty. He might want someone taking from A to B that no-one else should ken. Maybe a lady. Catching on, are we?

Me – Oh yes, right. Of course. Jeez, for a minute I thought he'd want me to sit outside a bank while he pulled a blag or something

Boss – Och no. Besides, he's got other people to do jobs like that for him. Joke! I'll get the sixty quid back to him right enough

Me – This was a test then. The "reason that will become apparent". You suspected he might test me because he's never seen me before

Boss – Aye. He knows me well enough but I couldn't do the hire today so he decided to test you

The following weekend Mr M did use my services as a driver and never used me again after that. It was a pretty boring, tedious and totally legal job in the end, rather than the glamorous lady I was expecting to sneak home for him. I was actually disappointed.

Not a Businessman

One sunny weekend afternoon, I was sat in my taxi outside the office engaged in yet another gripping round of Gem Drop. The funny thing about someone like me playing Gem Drop is that the object of the game is to line up different coloured gems and sparkly things to make them disappear before they're then promptly replaced by other jewels and shiny colours... and I'm colour blind. I am the worst colour blind person my optician has ever seen in his professional career he told me. In those Ishihara coloured dot tests you may have seen, I usually got around two out of fourteen correct, which wasn't good. So for me, Gem Drop was not only difficult, it was borderline impossible with some of the shades of red and green I had to try to distinguish to actually play the game. That aside, it passed the often-tedious periods when I had not much else to do on a nice sunny day after I'd cleaned the car out and checked oil levels… etc.

I got a call from the lady in the Spar to collect Woody and take him home. I asked if he had money, knowing who he was, and was told he had. I drove the short distance to the shop in the square and he climbed in looking utterly exhausted.

Me – Hi, Woody. You look knackered, mate

Woody – Aye, John, I'm fucked. Home, please. How much is it?

I told him and he paid me. Woody didn't use our taxis very much, but he looked like he wouldn't have made the short walk up the brae to his place that day. At that moment, Boss pulled up at the nearby junction and could see directly into my taxi. I was busy scribbling the details of the hire on the sheet when Woody tapped me on the shoulder. I looked up and to where he pointed, saw Boss, gave him a wee salute like we usually did when we 'eyeballed' one another on the road, and plopped the hire sheet clipboard back on the dash.

Woody – Where's Boss going?

Me – I've got no idea. He's off today

Woody (reaching for the hire sheet) – What's that you wrote down on that sheet?

Me (moving the sheet away from him) – Nothing to do with you, but basically I have to record all hires. Name, time, pick-up and destination. It the law, you see

Woody – Oh I didn't ken that

I pulled off to take Woody the short distance to his flat and, within a couple of minutes, I stopped right outside his door.

Me – There you go, Woody

Woody – Hey, I've had an idea

Me – OK, tell me

Woody – If you didn't write this hire on that sheet, you could take me home and pocket this money yourself. Clever, eh?

Me – Yes, Woody, very clever, but your cunning plan for worldwide financial domination has two very large flaws in it

Woody – Really? Go on then, tell me

Me – OK then. One. I'm not dishonest. Two, and this is the biggest flaw. Boss saw you in this very taxi not two minutes ago. You pointed him out to me. Remember? So, when I cash in at the end of the day and he doesn't see your name on the sheet at this time from the Spar to your flat. He will think, "Ooh hello. Lockett has ripped me off." Other than those two minor details it's a perfect plan. I might be colour blind, Woody, but I'm not stupid

Woody – If I was a taxi driver, I'd do it

Me – Yeah well, you're not and never will be. It's a shit job anyway. I keep getting punters in here telling me how I can rip my boss off, fail, and lose my job

Woody got out and slunk off home. I finished later that day and explained Woody's plan to Boss while I cashed in. He laughed and told me he'd already tested my honesty just after I first started and I successfully passed. Crafty move by Boss, but I think I would do the same.

Phone Top-Up

Julie and Tim were a middle-aged couple I knew quite well. They weren't very regular taxi customers, but when they did need a cab they used either us or Andy's, like a lot of people did. I also knew their son Mark who lived in Ayr, and he would often phone and ask us to go to his folks' house and get his mum to turn her mobile phone on. Apparently, she either kept turning it off or let the battery run out on a fairly regular basis. I think his dad was annoyed by, or didn't grasp, the whole situation to be honest, but Mark would drop in every so often to pay a wee slate we had running for this sole purpose. He phoned me up one day, like he had a few times before.

Me – Hello, T&C Taxis

Mark – Hi, John, it's Mark. Can you pop up to my folks please and ask Mum to turn the mobile on, please? No rush

Me – Sure. No problem, Mark

I locked up the office, then pootled over to his parents' house after I did a very quick local hire. Tim eventually came to the door after quite a lot of banging and crashing and commotion. He opened the door with immense difficulty because, unknown to me, he'd recently hurt his leg quite badly, and was therefore in a wheelchair with his damaged limb stuck out horizontally. He also couldn't open the door far enough for us to see each other properly and could only poke his heavily bandaged leg around the threshold, meaning that I spoke to his foot rather than to his face. A quite disconcerting experience.

Me – Hi, Tim. I'm John, the taxi driver

Tim (angrily) – What do you want?

Me – Your son Mark has asked me to come over. He would like you to turn your mobile phone on

Tim – What?

Me – It's turned off and he wants to talk to you

Tim (angrily) – What are you talking about?

Me – Is Julie in?

Tim (angrily) – No she is not. She's gone to the shop. What is all this nonsense?

Me – Oh. Sorry, Tim

I was in a bit of a pickle now, to be honest. Tim was angry and didn't seem to understand what I was talking about, and Julie wasn't home. I decided to call Mark up on the taxi phone, but just then, as if previously arranged, one of Andy's taxis pulled up behind mine and Julie climbed out. She ran over to me.

Me – Hi, Julie. Mark has called me. He wants you to turn your mobile on

Julie – OK, John, thanks. The battery ran flat and I had no credit so I just went down the shop to get a top-up. I walked to your office for a taxi but your place is locked up so I had to get one of Andy's

Me – Glad it's all sorted now

From behind the front door of the house, Tim could hear all of this, and was trying to jump up and down with rage even though he was in a wheelchair.

Tim – What on Earth is going on out there?! You've just got a taxi back from the shop and we've already got a taxi driver here?! What is going on Julie?!

I invented an urgent need to flee the scene and left.

Worst Party Ever

The rain fell heavily all day long one particular Sunday and never eased off, so my level of busyness didn't drop below astronomical, which suited me fine. More work meant more pay and tips, and the day passed more quickly. Not that I ever wanted to wish time away, but when you're sat in a Vauxhall Vectra for hour after hour, the day can't end soon enough. Late afternoon came and Natalie sent me to an address to pick up four young ladies and take them to their friend's house in Patna. I pulled up outside and pretty soon four heavily dolled up young ladies with plastic shopping bags covering up their hair scampered through the teeming rain into the taxi. They all carried clinking bags full of wine by the sound of it, too.

Me – Good afternoon, ladies

Lass 1 – Bloody hell, John. It's wet out there

After confirming their destination, we were soon on our merry way to Patna. The ladies chatted about this and that and the miles passed quickly enough. It turned out that one of them even had a key to the place, which was passed to the lass in the front seat at one point. The rain got worse and I soon pulled up outside their friend's house, whereupon they quickly clambered out once I'd been paid and scurried off up the path to the front door.

Being out of radio range, I opted to phone Natalie from where I was parked up. Very occasionally we would get a hire from Patna and I didn't want to waste a journey back to Dalmellington only to have to turn back round again. After a very brief chat with Natalie, I readied myself to pull off and head back to Dalmellington for a hire. The lass from the front seat moments ago was back and hammering on my passenger door. I wound the window down an inch and could see her three friends huddled under the very tiny canopy above the front door of the house looking utterly fed up.

Me – What's wrong?

Lass 1 – The key doesn't open the door, John. What do we do?

Me – Err... Where is your friend who lives here? Is she even in the house?

Lass 1 – We don't ken

Me – Phone her up

Lass 1 – We have, but she's not picking up

Me – Well maybe she's in the shower or something. Didn't you phone her before you came? Surely you arranged all this?

Lass 1 – It's a surprise party for her so we didn't arrange it. We thought she'd be in

Me – She'll be surprised finding her friends outside her door, soaking wet and with the wrong key to her house. Sorry, but I don't know what you want me to do

Lass 1 – Can you take us back to Dalmellington?

Me – Sure. Get in

They all piled back in the taxi again and after rebooking them back in via another quick call to Natalie, I dropped them off exactly where I'd picked them up from not ten minutes earlier. I found out later that they had copied the wrong key off their friend's house keys a week or so earlier. They were absolutely soaked and I think they forgot about the most badly organised surprise party in history and drank all the wine there instead.

We Are Not a Taxi Service

One very busy Saturday afternoon just as the pubs were closing. I was once again returning to the square from the direction of Main Street to pick up yet another punter. He was one of my favourite regulars and even though he tried to kiss me all the time he was tipsy, I totally enjoyed his company. As I approached the square I could see him bobbling about outside Peggy's, so I swung round the square to pick him up thinking "at least I haven't got to drag him out the pub this time".

I rounded the wee roundabout in the square and glanced down towards the taxi office for no particular reason and happened to notice a middle-aged lady called Penny who used our taxis from time to time stood outside our locked door. She saw me and waved but I was heading round the square, and anyway Ewan had already booked me. I stopped outside Peggy's, he climbed in and we were off. I figured to quickly get him home, then return to the office to get Penny which would only take me about five minutes. Boss wasn't around so I couldn't shout him to go and collect her either, but seeing as I'd saved a heap of time already by not having to hunt around the pub for Ewan, I thought no more of it.

Ewan was safely taken home and I swiftly returned to the

office to get Penny, whom I assumed would still be there. I pulled up outside and she was nowhere to be seen. I couldn't see Andy's guy parked up anywhere so I again made an assumption that Penny had either walked home or Andy had taken her. In either case I shrugged my shoulders, microwaved a coffee and eventually the incident, or lack of, had completely gone from my mind. Boss eventually showed up at around 5pm, cashed me in and I trundled off home.

The following morning was a typically quiet Sunday affair once I'd done my usual runs to here and there. While I slurped on a coffee, Boss busied himself under the bonnet of his taxi changing a headlight bulb. I held my hand out for him to deposit parts into and we chatted idly about this and that. I saw Penny walking along the pavement towards us and thought nothing of it whatsoever. She looked in a bad mood as she approached us.

Penny (pointing at me) – You fucker!

Me – What? Me? What are you on about, Penny?

Boss stood up, relocated his wee glasses onto the top of his head and eyed Penny with scorn.

Penny – You drove past me yesterday when I needed a taxi

Me – I did not

Penny – You fuckin' did, you liar. I was stood right here and I waved at you, but you drove round the square instead

I suddenly recalled the trivial details of this minor incident which Penny had obviously misunderstood. She folded her arms and her face contorted in rage.

Me – Aha! I was on my way to pick up someone else and couldn't get you then. I came back for you a few minutes later but you'd gone

Penny – You deliberately drove past me

Me – I drove round the square to get an already booked hire...

Boss (interrupting me) – ...so he couldn't get you

Penny – But I was stood right here waiting for you

Me – Aye, you may have been, but I had an already booked hire, and you weren't booked in, Penny. However, I did come back for you

Penny – This is awful

Boss – John was already booked for someone else. Understand?

Penny – Well, yes, but I was...

Boss – I don't think you do understand Penny. Go away and think about it before shouting your mouth off again

Me (trying a more diplomatic approach) – Why would I

deliberately not pick you up? That wouldn't make sense, would it? What if you were booked in for a hire, but I stopped to pick up someone else instead? You wouldn't like that

Penny – Who did you pick up before me?

Boss – What difference does that make? Bloody hell, Penny. You're being a bit silly over this. We are not a taxi service. I ken that sounds ridiculous but we're not. We operate private hire vehicles that have to be booked in, and someone else was booked in before you. John's hire was booked in before he even saw you, from what I can gather

Me – Aye they were

Boss – So there. Sorry, Penny, but if you have an issue with how we operate you'd better see the gaffer. Oh wait, that's me, and I'm backing my driver one hundred per cent

Penny walked off muttering under her breath and left Boss and myself to finish changing the headlight bulb. It did highlight the general public's lack of knowledge when it comes to taxis and private hire vehicles and the difference between them, however inconvenient or silly that may appear. It was a topic Boss and myself discussed from time to time and he was of the opinion that taxis and PHVs do the same job so should be treated the same. It's an opinion I broadly share, although I would only allow certain vehicles to be taxis, not just any four-door saloon. From my admittedly limited knowledge of the industry, I would only allow certain vehicles such as the traditional London black cab and equivalent vehicles (with wheelchair access and so on) to be taxis, leaving everything else to be a PHV/minicab. None of that would have meant that I would have picked Penny up before Ewan, however, and that was something that folk like Penny couldn't grasp.

Sale of the Century

Lez was a lad in his late twenties who I knew very well even though he didn't frequent our taxi services too often. Although he was fairly popular around the village, he often struggled to grasp how the world worked, as this story illustrates perfectly. On one particular Christmas, his mother bought him a cheap and basic mobile phone, which he sold to Boss for fifteen pounds a week or so later. The day after Boss bought the phone, Lez was back in the taxi office. I sat on a cluttered chair struggling with a tricky level of Gem Drop while Boss went through his endless mountain of confusing paperwork.

Lez – Morning, Boss

Boss – What is it, Lez? I'm very busy and in a very bad mood

Boss always said this to Lez and certain other individuals in an attempt to make them either go away or keep matters brief, but it rarely worked.

Lez – I need that phone back

Boss – Bit of tough shit there, Lez. I've sold it on. It's away

Lez – Fuck!

Me – Just buy another one, Lez

Lez – Aye very funny, John

Me – Err… What's funny about buying another phone?

Lez – Because I need that one back

Boss – Shouldn't have sold it then, Lez

Lez – I need it back, Boss

Boss – I've fuckin' sold it on, Lez!

Me – You following this, Lez?

Lez – Aye very funny (This was Lez's response to a lot of stuff.)

Me – I'm not trying to be funny, Lez. What's the big deal with this phone anyway? Just buy another. It was only a cheap wee thing, wasn't it? Nothing fancy

Lez – My mother bought it me for Christmas

Boss – So?

Lez – I shouldn't have sold it

Me – Well you have sold it and now Boss has sold it. End of situation, I'd say

Boss – Aye. Now fuck off, Lez

Lez exited the taxi office muttering about how unfair it was of Boss to sell the phone on, but the following day he was back.

Lez – Boss I really need that phone back. My mother will kill me

Boss – For fuck's sake, Lez. This is the last time I'm telling you. I've sold it on. It's away. Now FUCK OFF!

Me – Do you want me to write that down, Lez?

Lez – Aye very funny

Lez turned smartly out of the office and left me with a grumpy gaffer for the rest of the day. Why Boss even bought the phone off Lez in the first place baffled me, to be honest. I never even bummed Lez a cigarette because I learned very early on that the guy just did not grasp situations at all. He wanted the phone back, and even if it had been catapulted into the sun he would still want it back. Lez asked me for a cigarette once and I said "no". Lez explained that because he asked me for a cigarette *nicely*, I should give him one. I offered Lez a scenario where he goes into the bank and asks nicely for £1000 and see how far it got him. He didn't comprehend what I meant at all.

Me – Boss. You know he's just gonna keep coming back

Boss – Fuck him. I've sold the phone on

Me – I don't think Mr Lez is fully grasping that, Boss

Boss – I'll fuckin' grasp him if he comes in here again about that phone

The next day and the relentless Lez approached the taxi office. I could tell by his facial expression that it was absolutely no problem to return and ask for the phone back yet again.

Me – Boss. Lez is coming

Boss – Fuck's sake. If it's about that phone I'm gonna fuckin' blow up

Lez entered and I cringed inwardly at what would soon transpire.

Lez – Boss, I need that phone back

Boss explained to Lez in a calm and collected manner, occasionally referring to some prepared notes and helpful diagrams (not really) that the phone could not be returned to him on account that someone else was now the rightful owner. Lez nodded and rubbed his chin a few times. He now seemed to comprehend the situation, but then uttered a sentence which dashed all hope to the ground.

Lez – So, when can I have it back then?

Boss stepped away quickly and went outside.

Me – Lez. Listen. It seems that this phone has been sold on by Boss. You understand?

Lez – Aye. Of course I understand

Me – I don't think you do, mate. How do you expect Boss to get it back?

Lez – I need it back

Me – Lez, I don't think you understand. Boss has sold the phone on to someone else. Following this, are we?

Lez – Aye. I'm not thick

Me – Ahem. OK, now just go away and buy another phone like the one your mother got you

Lez – I haven't got any money

Me – Oh Lez, for pity's sake, man. It was only a cheap phone. Not a brand-new state-of-the-art job. Just a basic phone. You'll get one for twenty quid. You get more than that every week in your benefits

Lez – Aye but I spend it on scratchcards and fags

For reasons unknown to myself I persevered with trying to explain to Lez that he just needed to go and buy another phone. Any phone would do too. I even pointed him in the direction of a local guy who would flog him a cheap used phone for about ten pounds, but it was wasted effort.

Me – You're not in charge of a major bank, are you? Or Chancellor?

Lez – Aye very funny

Me – Look just fuck off and stop bothering Boss about the bloody phone

Lez stepped outside and Boss returned after a very brief, vocal and animated exchange with Lez on the pavement. He looked utterly exhausted and irate.

Boss – I'm gonna get that phone back. I'll sell it back to Lez for twenty quid and at least it will stop the daft sod coming back. Plus, I'll make a fiver

Me – Probably a wise move, Boss

I didn't work on the particular Sunday the deal went down, so I missed it. Boss explained the details to me the following Monday morning, then shortly after we had finished our school runs, Lez was in our wee office once more.

Lez – Boss, I'll get you the rest of that money by Wednesday when I get my money

Boss – OK, Lez. Another tenner and you get the phone back

Lez had already given Boss ten pounds towards the phone, which Boss has managed to get back, somehow, although he probably never sold it on to anyone else in the first place and just kept it as a spare or 'burner' phone. Lez went away, our lives returned to normal for a while, but he returned the following morning. Boss peered at him over his pound-shop reading glasses.

Lez – Boss, I need that tenner back

Boss erupted and the cheap specs went flying across the room.

Me – Fuckin' hell, Lez. How do you manage all this bollocks that goes on in that brain of yours?

Boss (rummaging in his wallet for a ten-pound note) – Here, Lez. Take this tenner and get to fuck out of my taxi office NOW!

Lez – I'll get the money by the end of the week

Boss – You'll get fuck all, laddie! I'm gonna jump up and down on that phone

Lez exited rapidly and I retrieved Boss's glasses from the floor.

Me – That phone you bought off Lez is turning out to be a total pain in the arse. I can't believe you even entered into a deal with him in the first place

Boss – Aye. I wish I hadn't bought the bloody thing now. I thought that even Lez would understand the basics of how the deal would work. Oh well. I'm past caring now, John. Whatever happens, will happen. I'll leave it at that

Boss drove off in his car to attend to some chores and I was shortly joined by Natalie who took over the phone and radio.

Natalie – Oh I see Lez coming. I wonder what he wants?

Me – I can guess

Natalie – He been in already has he?

Me – Aye. He sold Boss a phone but wants it back. He's now started paying Boss for the phone but now needs the money back

Natalie – Och deary me, eh

Lez entered, nodded at me then turned his attention to Natalie who was already trying to ignore him by busying herself in paperwork.

Lez – Where's Boss?

Me – In Ayr getting Vauxhall parts

Lez – I want to give him this tenner towards the phone

Me – Lez, you were in here less than an hour ago wanting the tenner back, for pity's sake!

Lez – Aye well Boss said he was gonna jump up and down on the phone

Me – Well, I don't know what to say

Natalie (glancing up) – Sounds like you're in another mess, Lez

Lez – Aye

Lez offered Natalie a tenner.

Lez – Give this to Boss, Nat

Natalie – Lez, I don't want to get involved. John has told me about the situation and it's between you and Boss. I want nothing to do with it

Me – Aye, Lez. Don't involve Natalie in all this pish

Lez – Just take the tenner, Natalie

Natalie – No, Lez. You'll have to see Boss later

Lez gave in and swiftly left. The day went fairly normally after that and I actually thought that the Great Phone Fiasco was over when after a number of days I heard no more about it off Boss or Lez himself. I wondered how it had been resolved and was on the verge of asking Boss what the outcome was, when a few days later Lez came back in the office around 10am. There was just myself and Natalie.

Lez – Where's Boss? I've just seen him drive off in a taxi

Me – How odd for a taxi driver to drive off in a taxi. We must call the authorities

Lez – Aye very funny

Natalie – He's gone to Kilmarnock, Lez

Lez – When will he be back?

Natalie – After two

Lez – I've got the money for that phone. Can I give it you, Natalie?

Natalie – Is that phone business still going on? Jeez! I'll phone Boss. Hold on, Lez

Natalie phoned Boss, and while they talked, I engaged Lez in a bit of chit-chat.

Me – Lez, old chap. Bit of advice for you, mate. Either sort this phone thing out today or forget about it. Understand? It has gone on long enough and Boss is getting a wee bit baked off with all this messing about. He's my gaffer and I don't want him annoyed anymore, OK?

Lez – Aye, OK

Me – It had better be "aye OK" Lez. You don't seem to understand how much grief you've caused with all this. Mind you, Boss should've known better than to do any kind of deal with you in the first place

Natalie finished her call with Boss and stared intently at Lez.

Natalie – I'll take the money but Boss has got the phone with him. You'll have to come back after 2pm

Amazingly, Lez agreed to this plan and left after giving Natalie the cash but was promptly back in the office around noon. My immediate thought was that he suddenly remembered he needed twenty pounds for some cigarettes or scratchcards or something equally as banal.

Lez – Where's Boss?

Natalie – I told you he won't be back until after 2pm, Lez

Lez – Aye you did. I've been to the dentist and I'm all doped up

Me – You're dopey enough, mate

Lez – Aye very funny

Natalie – Have you come for the money back or something?

Lez – No

Me – You sure, Lez? You don't need it to go and blow it on scratchcards or fags or a nag in the three-thirty race at Kempton Park?

Lez – No

Once again, Lez departed and returned around 2pm

Lez – Where's Boss?

Natalie – He won't be long, Lez. He has to be back here by 2.20pm anyway for the school-kid runs

Lez waited while I enjoyed some Gem Drop and Natalie fought a losing battle with paperwork. Boss came in around 2.15pm looking more fed up than usual and totally ignored Lez who stood with his hand held out expecting the phone within seconds of Boss's arrival. Boss eventually finished with his mail and various other time-wasting exercises purely designed to frustrate Lez. He gathered the phone up with the charger before finally striding over to Lez and plonking them in his outstretched hands.

Boss – Here's the phone back. Don't ever come back here and

try to sell me anything ever again, or even try to scrounge one penny or a cigarette or anything at all. There's the door, now piss off and shut it from the other side

Lez swiftly departed and thankfully that was the end of the matter. I half expected him to try to resell the phone back to Boss, but miraculously, and to Boss's relief, we never had him peddling anything again.

Geography

As yet another day slowly eased by, I eventually pulled up outside one of the local primary schools to begin my school runs. All the usual folk were there picking up their children and I casually leant against my taxi gazing at nothing in particular while I waited. There was a small group of mothers waiting for their kids, and one or two of them waved at me and I gave a wee wave in return. Then one of them beckoned me over.

Lady 1 – John, come here

I sauntered over to her thinking that she maybe wanted a taxi later and was going to book it with me there and then, so I took the booking sheet with me.

Me – Afternoon, ladies

Lady 1 – Do you ken where Balmedie is, John?

Me (rubbing my chin) – No, sorry. Never heard of the place

Lady 2 (amazed) – What do you mean "Never heard of the place"?

Me – Ahem. I mean the name isn't familiar to me. I've never heard of it. I don't know where it is and I don't think it's local

Lady 2 – Not local?

Me – I'm sorry, but I've never heard of it. Is it a village or the name of a farm?

Lady 1 – It's a village

Me – No, I still can't place it. I know most places around here now. I even know where Gass is and I think that's the smallest place on any map I've ever come across

Lady 2 – Gass? Where's that?

Me – It's between Dalmellington and Straiton

Lady 1 – Don't ken the place

Lady 2 – Never heard of it

Me – What do you mean "Never heard of it"?

Lady 2 (laughing) – Och you cheeky so and so

Me – This Balmedie place. Why are you asking about it? What's the story?

Lady 1 – It's near Aberdeen and I thought you might ken it

Me – Aberdeen is about two hundred miles away! How on Earth would I know a village that far away? Would an Aberdeen taxi driver know where Gass was? You don't, and it's only a few miles up the road

Lady 1 – I thought you taxi drivers were smart and knew this kind of stuff

Me – I'm not Google Maps, you know

I ambled back to my taxi, resumed my leaning posture and pondered why on Earth they were asking me about a place that was two hundred miles away. I gave up trying to reason why and didn't even want to ask them. If I was as smart as she thought I was, I wouldn't be driving a Vauxhall for a living.

Mrs Puzzolenta

On one of the many varied parcel rounds I used to cover, I had a delivery for an address I hadn't been to before in the poshest part of Ayr. Sorry, not Ayr... Alloway... Oh yes, Alloway. It borders Ayr at the southern end but a lot of folks there insist it has nothing to do with Ayr at all. I knocked on the door of the very posh and expensive-looking house and a very smartly dressed lady in her mid-forties soon greeted me as I held out the wee parcel. She spoke with a light Scottish accent.

Me – Parcel for a Mrs Puzzolenta

Mrs Puzzolenta – Thank you

She took the wee package and signed my gadget.

Me – Nice name. Puzzolenta. Sounds exotic

Mrs Puzzolenta (frowning) – I beg your pardon?

Me – Your surname. Puzzolenta. Sounds interesting. Exotic. Nice

Mrs Puzzolenta (frowning a wee bit more now) – I honestly don't know what you mean

Me – Well, my surname is Lockett and that's kind of average, I suppose. My mate is a Smith and he hates it because it's so "ordinary" as he puts it. Puzzolenta sounds exciting and adventurous. Italian, I imagine

Mrs Puzzolenta (folding her arms and glaring now) – I have absolutely no idea what you are going on about young man. Good day

With that, she turned smartly on her expensive shoes and slammed her front door. I shrugged and finished my round, then returned back to base later that day. Boss was fiddling about on his computer and we started chatting. I went in the wee kitchen to make a fresh and much-needed coffee.

Boss – The usual boring parcel round, Lockett?

Me – Yeah, although there was a lady in Alloway I upset

Boss – Oh Alloway, eh? You didn't say it was in Ayr, did you? They hate that

Me – No, I just happened to make a remark about her surname and that I liked it

Boss – What's her surname?

Me – Puzzolenta

Boss – Ooh sounds nice. Italian, I'd think

Me – That's what I said. Exotic and interesting

Boss – I'll google it. I bet it's the Italian for something weird and she doesn't like it

Boss googled 'Puzzolenta' after I spelled it out for him by referring back to my gadget.

Boss – Google is asking if I mean 'Puzzolente' with an 'e' instead of "a" at the end

Me – Aye that will do

He clicked on Puzzolente and shortly erupted with laughter.

Boss – Oh Lockett you fool. "Nice name you've got there, Mrs

Puzzolenta". Ha ha

Me – Why? What does it mean?

Boss – Puzzolente, which is one letter different, means "smelly".
"Ooh nice name you have there, Mrs Smelly"

Me – Oh, bollocks

Obviously, the lady's name was nothing like Puzzolenta/e. I
have used that as an example, but her name was just one letter
different from something not very pleasant, which may explain
her reaction, and she must have thought I was trying to be a
smart arse.

Cheek!

Any business in any industry likes to take care of good
customers, and the taxi business is no different. Favours and
errands and 'going the extra mile', in some cases literally, were
the things we did for a variety of folks and the vast majority
appreciated it very much. Regular customers like Ron and Joan
with their numerous trips down to the shops and fairly regular
trips to Kate's in Ayr, were folk we tried to take care of as much
as we could. They did take advantage of Boss's leniency with
them, however.

Boss was in the office one day, doing paperwork and
handling the phone. I was sat in the taxi and may have been
playing Gem Drop and pretty soon he shouted me over the
radio.

Boss – TC6, instead of wasting your life playing that stupid phone game, go and get a bottle of Glen's vodka and twenty Superkings and take them up to Ron and Joan. It's all on their slate

Me – Roger

I swiftly dealt with that, and the rest of the day went pretty much as normal. Then I spied Joan go past our office in Andy's taxi. They used us to get them booze and fags on credit, and I know they won't pay it back for ages, then use Andy's taxis! The cheek of it! So, I informed Boss who promptly exploded.

Boss (taking off his glasses, which meant he was deadly serious) – Right then. If either of them dopey sods want anything at all on credit they can fuck right off. If they've got money, then OK

Me – Aye, Boss, quite right. Cheeky pair, they are

Boss – They're the fuckin' limit. The running around we do for them. The favours and everything else. Fuck's sake!

A few days passed then Ron phoned up while I was on duty alone.

Ron – Oh hello, John. Is Boss there?

Me – No, Ron. He's in Ayr getting car parts. I'll get him to call you back later, OK?

Ron – It's about the other day

Me – OK Ron. I'll tell him

Which I did upon Boss's return and he promptly exploded, before he popped round to Ron and Joan's after a wee phone call with them, while I stood outside the office watching the village go by. He soon returned looking very serious, got out his taxi and ambled over to me.

Boss – Well, I've laid it on the line to them. We'll see if their brains can cope with that

Me – We'll see, eh Boss

Another day or so passed and Ron phoned up, but yet again Boss wasn't around.

Ron – Is Boss there?

Me – No Ron. He's in Ayr getting car parts I think. Shall I get him to call you back?

Ron – Yes. Tell him I've got something here for him. Personal stuff

Me – OK, Ron, I'll tell him

On Boss's return, I gave him the message and he went and paid Ron a visit after I finished later that day. I came in the next morning desperate to hear the latest developments.

Me – Morning, Boss

Boss – Morning, John

Me – What did Ron want you for yesterday?

Boss – He gave me the money he owed us. All of it. He also told me that they'll be using Andy's taxis instead of us from now on

Me – Oh. It's a pity really because apart from all the fucking about they were decent customers

Boss – Aye, but I can't be doing with getting fucked about like those pair of clowns. They'll be back within a week anyway. Andy doesn't really allow a slate and if he does he'll charge them a fortune. He won't entertain their pish for long either

A few days passed, the taxi phone rang and I could immediately see it was Ron.

Ron – Is Boss there?

Me – Hi, Ron. Unbelievably he's down in Ayr getting car parts

Ron – Oh, can you ask him to phone me? We need to talk

Me – Aye Ron, I will

I immediately guessed what Ron wanted to talk with Boss about, so I phoned him up. He was at home, not getting car parts at all and I told him that Ron wanted a 'chat'. I could almost see Boss's insane grin appear on the mobile's wee screen.

Boss – I fuckin' told you they'd be back. Ron with a grovelling apology, I have no doubt

Boss drove down to the taxi office shortly after he'd been for a wee chat with Ron. He explained to me that Andy had ripped Ron off, which I doubted very much to be honest, and will we have them back as customers again! I should imagine that Andy tired very quickly of their pish and told them in no uncertain terms. Over the years I worked for Boss I had no dealings with Andy whatsoever, and the sum total of my conversations with him would amount to a few sentences. I never had any need to converse with him about anything, other than a few occasions when we split twenty-pound notes or whatever. He always struck me as a no-nonsense kind of guy much like Boss was, which probably explained why Dalmellington's two taxi chiefs didn't get along. I could easily see why Ron and Joan would quickly get on his nerves and wasn't in the least bit surprised at this latest turn of events. In every situation that arose, like this state of affairs, Boss was always proven right.

Potatoes

Mr S was a big burly man who despite his fearsome looks, strongman physique and towering height was a decent guy who never gave me or anyone else any aggravation as far as I know. He didn't look the sort of guy you'd want to mess with though. I got on with him well enough, and we shared a connection with the city of Sheffield. My mother was born there, and so was he, which meant his accent constantly reminded me of the place.

I picked him up from a local shop one day and we filled the boot of the taxi with bags of groceries. I parked up at the end of the path to his house and we both proceeded to carry bags down the path to the door where he plonked them down, opened the house door, shouted his son to come and help, then returned back to the car for more bags. It should be noted that the house was lower than the road by quite a way and there were a good number of steps down to it. His lad Jack, who was about twenty years old, appeared and stood in the doorway with his hands in his pockets. He was a bit of a feckless youth and I think his dad had tried to toughen him up, but it didn't seem to be working. He was thin and pasty and quite sickly looking to my eyes.

Jack – Hi, John

Me – Hi, Jack. You OK, bud?

Jack – Aye not too bad

By this time, Mr S was back at the taxi removing the last of the shopping as I placed a couple of bags down by the door. I turned and could see Mr S holding a big 25kg bag of potatoes above his head with ease.

Mr S – My lad could never do this, John. Look at him. All thin and weedy. You need toughening up, son

Jack – Oh Dad, give it a rest

I started my way up the steps back to the car, and Mr S launched the bag at this son.

Mr S – Catch!

His son was hit square in the chest and, screaming loudly, was thrown violently back into the house and onto the floor, with potatoes rolling everywhere from the burst bag. I went back down to help but thankfully couldn't see any damage done, and was waved away by Mrs S who assured me that Jack would be fine. He groaned a wee bit then sat up from his flattened position rubbing his chest.

Mr S – You wimp!

Mrs S (at Mr S) – You idiot!

I made my excuses and left.

Cauliflower

I had nicknames for a lot of my regulars, like I imagine a lot of people do in many walks of life. Not derisory names or anything negative. They were just a marker I used in my own head. One such gentleman I named Mr Cauliflower or Colly. He moaned to me one day that the local Co-op didn't have any cauliflowers so he phoned Co-op headquarters in Manchester and complained "most severely" about it. I liked the old guy in a "miserable old bloke" way to be honest. He trod on a landmine when he served in the army in his youth and walked with a wee limp ever since, but wasn't very popular around the village, seemed very awkward around people and tended to sit alone in the pub. He spoke with a rough Lancashire accent and had lived in Dalmellington since retiring many years previously.

A few days before one particular Christmas, he slipped over on some ice while he was delivering cards to his neighbours at 3am. Yes, 3am. He broke his hip and right thigh bone and spent a year getting fixed up with various operations so, consequently, he didn't require our services as much, although we did favours and ran a newspaper and occasional messages round to him. It was the January just over twelve months later we first started getting him again for his daily taxi hire down the shop and back, and his twice-a-week jaunt to the Railway pub.

Things were going well, then his wife was admitted to a local nursing home when she fell gravely ill. This was when it all started to go wrong. He drove Boss, myself and everyone else round the bend with his manner and conduct. He was never a horrible man, and we all had a wee soft spot for him, but he didn't seem to possess any social skills or empathy.

He would phone Boss at 6 or 7am and ask for a taxi at 9am which we couldn't do because of the school runs. After a brief chat, a time of 9.10am would be agreed. But the annoying thing was we would have to go through the same tiresome rigmarole every day. He could never comprehend why we couldn't pick him up at 9am. Either that or he was just deliberately awkward.

In the mornings, we would all set off and do our regular taxi runs to various schools and so on. Then whoever was back around the 9am mark, which was usually Boss would collect

Colly and take him to the nursing home to visit his missus. All nice and normal you would think, but Colly would phone about half a dozen times or more since 7am to check, and recheck, that he'd booked a taxi for 9.10am. It got so bad we stopped answering the phone if his name showed on it. He booked a taxi with me one day, watched me write it down on the booking sheet, then still phoned back to check ten minutes later.

After we successfully dropped him off at the nursing home we usually got a call asking us to pick him up around the 10am mark. We would collect him and drop him off at the shop opposite the Railway. He would spend about ten minutes in the shop getting a few items, then stand in the shop waiting for the pub to open at 11am. I could never understand why he didn't rearrange his morning timings and either go to the home later or leave the home for the shop nearer to 11am.

The shop eventually tired of his antics and hunted him out, which simply meant that he then started hanging around outside the pub wanting in before 11am, and moaned when they wouldn't open the doors. This led to him sitting in the café down the street nursing a cup of tea until near 11am, then racing straight to the Railway until he was blootered around school-finishing time. Inevitably he would phone for a taxi while we're on one of our busiest period of the day getting kids home. No other person in the entire village had any trouble understanding that they couldn't get a taxi during the two periods a day when we were either taking kids to school or home. In fact, I think most folks admired our total refusal to do any other hires that may jeopardise our school runs. A typical exchange would go like this when he eventually got in the car.

Colly – Hi, John

Me – Hello, Mr C

Colly – I couldn't get a taxi at 3pm. Boss said I had to wait

Me (knowing what his answer would be) – Well, you could use Andy's taxis. He doesn't do school runs. Or use Karl's taxis

Colly – Fuck Andy, and fuck Karl as well

Me – We've got school kids around the 3pm mark every weekday Mr C. You know that

Colly – School kids?

Me – Aye. Small people. They go to school. You must have heard of them

Colly – Aye

This state of affairs went on for a wee while until his missus sadly passed away. Colly was in the Railway when I got a call from the pub and I swiftly collected him within about two minutes and ran the poor old guy down to the nursing home in total silence. He looked very upset and the last thing he would want to hear would be my inane drivel. Less than an hour later, I received a call from the home, and I knew who it would be before I picked up so I put on my serious voice.

Me – Good afternoon. T&C Taxis

Lady at the Home – Can we have a taxi for Mr C, please?

Me – Of course. Is he going home?

Lady at the Home – He won't say

Me – Well, I know his wife has just passed on, but I need to know where he's going. He may want to go to Ayr or somewhere else distant

Lady at the Home – I'll ask him

I heard the lady ask Colly but he wasn't forthcoming. Just a brief "get me a taxi" comment.

Lady at the Home – He won't tell me, I'm afraid

Me – I'll be there in two minutes

A brief jaunt to the home and I was joined by the very sad and distraught Colly.

Me – So, Mr C. Where are we going? The lady on the phone wouldn't tell me

Colly – Aye. I wouldn't tell her. I didn't want her to know

Me – Oh. Why is that? I need to know where you're going, Mr C

Colly – I'm going back to the pub

Me – Oh

I took him back to the pub, by which time everyone in the entire village had found out the sad news of Mrs C's passing. As I pulled up outside the Railway, the three locals who were stood outside gasped in incredulity at Colly's arrival less than one hour after he had left.

After a short while, Colly moved out of his house into a sheltered accommodation complex in the village and still used our taxis virtually every day. He continued to try to book a car just as the schools were finishing too. This meant we couldn't accommodate him and we engaged in protracted negotiations with him regarding pick-up times. In actual fact, the local high school-finishing time varied every day between 2.40pm and 3.30pm which made matters even more complicated. Add in the other major factor that the four local primary schools all finished at 3pm, and the added complication that brothers and sisters may be at different schools many miles apart and finishing at wildly different times, meant that our afternoon school runs were very time consuming and tricky logistical headaches and lasted from approximately 2.30 to 4pm. However, these arrangements went on for quite some time, and despite Colly's total unwillingness to understand that the school-kid runs were our absolute top priority, everything ran fairly smoothly.

Then one day Colly called at about 10am for a taxi to take him to the Railway at 11am. I wrote the details down on the hire sheet like I had done thousands of times before then carried on with some other hires until about 10.59am when I drove the short distance to the home. It was absolutely throwing it down with rain and parking outside the home was impossible as usual so I pulled up about twenty yards past the entrance. I looked back over my left shoulder and could see the curtain on the glass panel at the side of the main entrance twitch a few times.

I assumed Colly was waiting for a break in the rain, which wasn't going to happen. The sky was black and it had been tipping it down all morning. I waited and glanced back occasionally at the twitching curtain while I muttered "come on Colly" to myself a few times. The curtain kept twitching and the rain kept on falling but Colly didn't emerge. Deciding to go and "carry his bag", thinking that maybe he hadn't spotted the taxi, I dashed the few yards through the rain and opened the door. Loudly exclaiming woe at the relentless downpour, I shook some droplets off my cap, but Colly still twitched the curtain and peered through the rain-streaked glass.

Me – It's a bit wet today, Mr C

Colly – You're fuckin' late. I've phoned Andy's taxi up now. You can fuck off

I looked at my watch and it was 11.02am and I'd spent probably two minutes parked up outside waiting for him to emerge.

Me – Late? How can I be late when I set off at 10.59 from a hundred yards away, sat in the car waiting for two minutes and it's only 11.02 now?

Colly – Well you are and I'm not using your taxis again, big 'un. I'll use Andy from now on

Me – Well that's your decision, Mr C, but I must admit I'm a bit surprised at your, may I say, rash decision considering the help we have all given you over the years. Not forgetting favours like when we moved that television for you... and when we get your newspapers... and when we...

Colly (cutting me off) – Help? I can never get a taxi at three in the afternoon when I want one

Me – I think we've covered that, Mr C. School kids. They are our priority

Colly – Yes, you keep telling me. I'm sick of hearing it

Me – I'm sorry to hear that, Mr C. I hope you get better service from Andy. Goodbye

I stepped quickly back to my taxi and carried on with the rest of my day until a few minutes before 3pm, or whatever time it was that particular day, when I parked up at the school to collect the first of my school kids and Boss rolled up behind me. I got out my car and sauntered over, passing him that day's hire sheet where I had crossed through Colly's 11am hire and made an explanatory note by it. Boss peered at it.

Boss (incredulous) – You are joking

Me – Sadly not, Boss. He was quite adamant that I was late and we're no help to him whatsoever. Also, he couldn't even have had time to phone for Andy because he was stood just inside the doorway when I arrived

Boss explained that Colly would get no joy whatsoever from Andy with his constant mithering, and within a few weeks Colly was once again a regular customer. He still complained when he couldn't get a taxi at 3pm, except in the school holidays. But that always made the situation worse in some ways because he would then explain that he *could* get taxis at 3pm during school holidays, so why can't he have one when he wants just because the kids are at school.

Loyalty

Without conducting an extensive survey of the people I used to pick up in my taxi, I didn't exactly know how many of them used our services exclusively, or if they used whichever of the village's two, and later on three, cab outfits they felt like. I had a whole host of regular customers that usually filled up the entire day, and if I was extremely busy, I would often see one of my usual customers in Andy's taxi, and to be honest, it never bothered me in the slightest. Why would it? They needed a taxi and I was too busy at that moment so they used someone else. It made perfect sense to me, and I would have done the exact same thing.

As I drove around the village throughout the day, I would occasionally pass one of Andy's drivers going in the opposite direction, and out of plain human curiosity I would have a wee glance at who was in the passenger seat. Many times, it was someone I had never had in my cab, and the sheer number of times I had the same people in my taxi day after day made me conclude that a great number of people were either Boss or Andy regulars. This changed somewhat when Karl started his enterprise up, but we kept a large percentage of our hardened regulars.

I tried my utmost to look after all my customers, whether they were an almost daily regular, or a 'once in a blue moon' passenger. As Boss used to say, "A new customer today, could be the regular of tomorrow," and he was right. I treated everyone the same even though I may have had favourites or people I would rather have in my cab than some other folks.

Cold and wet weather meant I was much busier than if it was warm and dry, and one particular weekday the rain started in the early afternoon and came down so hard and continuous I thought it would never end. Before the downpour, I had taken a number of hires all over the village, including Adam, who was one of the oldest guys in Dalmellington. He told me, and I had no reason to disbelieve him, that he only ever used our taxis because he liked Boss and didn't get along with Andy at all. I had dropped Adam off at the Black Bull just after opening time like I did twice a week for a very long time. He was that regular, he was one of the very few who had his booking to go to the pub pre-printed on the daily hire sheet. His return journey home could vary so he always used to stand outside the pub and we knew that he then wanted to go home, or he would totter over the road to our office and wait in the luxurious comfort of our waiting room if it was unlocked. He was the nicest and most polite man I had the pleasure to drive anywhere, but I exclusively took him to the Bull and back home again.

The afternoon wore on and the rain kept on falling. I didn't think the inky black clouds above could hold any more water but they just kept on pouring with rain and never once let off all afternoon long. Boss was outside the village either on a day off or doing some repairs in the workshop, so I just soldiered on by myself ferrying wet and weary people to all manner of places. After the Bull closed its doors for the day, I knew Adam would want a cab home but I had a few more hires to complete before I could get to him.

All this time, Andy's taxi was empty, which I found very unusual considering the appalling weather, and its driver was chatting with a guy in Peggy's doorway. I drove past our office during the last of that string of hires and I caught sight of Adam desperately trying to keep out of the pouring rain under our extremely tiny canopy over the office doorway. I could see he was already soaking wet, and with the rain driving in at an angle he would get wetter and wetter the longer he stayed there. Dropping my current hire off in record time, I quickly turned around and headed back to the office and Adam bundled himself in the passenger seat. He looked absolutely drowned and very miserable.

Me – Sorry I couldn't get to you earlier, Adam

Adam – No problem, John

I pointed to Andy's taxi which was parked outside Peggy's, and clearly visible from our office.

Me – You should have used Andy's taxi. He's hasn't had a hire for a while now

Adam – John, I will never use Andy's taxis. I told you that a long time ago and I meant it. I like Boss and you

Me – We appreciate your loyalty but you're soaking wet. I don't like to see you like this, Adam

Adam – You and Boss are very kind to me. That's why I use your taxis and not Andy's. I will never use anyone else's taxis, John

I took him home and walked him to his door like I always did. He thanked me once again and I drove off to yet another hire in the teeming downpour that hadn't eased one iota since it began. I remarked on what Adam said to me when I met up with Boss later and he told me he has known Adam all his life and wasn't in the least bit surprised. He also told me he had known Adam wait for one of our taxis for over an hour on some occasions instead of using Andy's, even if it meant a major inconvenience to himself. In conclusion, I decided that although we had many regulars, and a good number of those would often choose us over Andy's taxi. Only Adam would *never* use anyone else and boy did he mean it.

Bloody Boots

I had been picking Karen up for some time over the years when one day I got a call to go and collect her from her mother's house and take her home: a routine hire I had done many times, and we always had a wee laugh over her boyfriend's latest exploits that she enjoyed relaying to me. Karen was an attractive and very likeable young lady in her mid-twenties and her lovely wee daughter, Jen, who was about six years old, was often with her. In contrast, her boyfriend Scott was a herbert of the highest order and was often in trouble with the law for a never-ending stream of trivial offences, which eventually resulted in him wearing an ankle tag. He promptly cut it off and microwaved it, nearly burning the kitchen down, he gleefully explained to me one day.

I remember one telling incident when I took Karen and Jen to one of the local shops and we came across Scott who was stood outside.

Me – Oh look, it's your beloved boyfriend

Karen – Jeez! I wonder what he's hanging around here for?

Me – Maybe he's planning to help an old lady across the road

Karen – Aye right. To the bank with her PIN number probably. Why can't he just behave himself?

Karen paid me, and she got out with her daughter who walked straight up to her dad and looked up at him as he puffed on a cigarette, eyeing everything around him with disdain. I had my windows down and could hear everything.

Jen – Daddy

Scott – What do you want, wee 'un?

Jen – Why can't you behave yourself like me and Mummy instead of being naughty all the time?

Karen – Come on, Jen. Your dad is obviously very busy. Leave him be, eh

Jen – He's so naughty, Mummy

Karen – Yes, we ken he is. Come on now

Scott just ignored her. I must admit I did have a wee inward chuckle at a six-year-old telling her dad off like that.

Back to the current hire, and I dutifully pulled up and waited for Karen outside her mother's house. She emerged alone, with a huge bandage on her right foot. It was the sort of bandage I'd only ever seen on cartoon characters. It was massive and obviously brand new, yet Karen made swift progress down the short pathway and climbed in the taxi easily enough as I held the door for her. I then got in and started the engine while I stared blatantly at her bandage.

Me – Hi, Karen. That looks painful

Karen – You will not believe this, John, but I ken you quite well and this will make you sick. I'll tell you when we get to my house

Me – Your chap hasn't hurt you, has he?

Karen – No, he hasn't. I'll tell you when we've stopped at mine

We arrived at Karen's a short while later and I switched the engine off. She looked at me.

Karen – You ken my wee lassie, Jen? She wouldn't hurt a fly, would she?

Me – No, she wouldn't Karen. She strikes me as a very pleasant wee lass. A credit to you

I was going to remark on how well she'd brought Jen up considering her chap's prevalence for bad behaviour, but thought better of it.

Karen – She's a wee bit scared of her dad and even though he's never hurt her, or me, she's still very wary of him

Me – I understand

Karen – She found some broken glass in the back garden. I think it was the remains of a pane from the shed or something. It had been broken ages although she didn't break it. Anyway, she was scared of what her dad might say, so she hid it

Me – Go on

Karen – You ken those knee length boots I've got? Or rather had, I should say

Me – Yes. Nice boots

Karen – I went to put them on the other day. They're really tight so I have to push down hard to get my foot in, and I was in agony when my foot finally slid in. Absolute screaming agony. I couldn't get the boot off quick enough. Luckily my mate was at my house and she pulled it off. Blood everywhere. And a huge shard of broken glass pointing upwards right into my sole

Me – Bloody hell, Karen

Karen – I'm OK now. A few stitches and nothing serious. Bloody hell, it hurt though

Me – I can't imagine the pain you must have felt. What about Jen? Does she know what's happened? Or have you made up a story? She'll be upset if she thinks she has hurt her own mother

Karen – Oh, I told her some story about spraining my ankle on a kerb. She was at my mother's at the time. I just wish she'd have hidden the glass in Scott's boot

Five a Day

Regular is a word that would describe many of our customers. Regular could mean once a day like the sunrise, or once every seventy-odd years like Halley's Comet, but it normally covers events that happen often with no uneven time intervals between occurrences. This wee tale concerns a woman called Shirley and she was very regular. Five-times-in-one-day regular on one occasion.

She phoned up for a taxi one day and because I was just loafing in the office, probably playing Gem Drop, I went and picked her up straight away. I parked up outside her house and within seconds she was sprinting down the drive as she always did for some reason I could never establish. I wish every hire would have been as keen as Shirley was. The number of times I'd pull up outside an address at the appointed time, only to be met with my hire shouting "two minutes" or "hang on a bit, John" at me was a source of minor tedium. I even had one guy sprint down the path covered in shaving foam to tell me I was a few minutes early. Well, I'll wait then. Sheesh!

I mentioned in my previous book how I had one instance of the most common taxi-driving events. Spewing up, violence, someone running off without paying and that kind of thing. In all my years of cabbing, there was just one guy who was actually ready every time I went to pick him up. He would time the short walk from his front door as I appeared into view so that he was actually opening the door to my cab as I gently eased the taxi to a halt. He was like a machine, that guy. Anyway, Shirley got in my taxi in a flurry of fluster and self-created panic like she always did.

Me – Hi, Shirley

Shirley – Hello, John. Sorry if I'm being a bother

Me – Not at all, Shirley. It's my job and you're not a bother at all

This little exchange happened every time I picked her up. She somehow thought that phoning up for a taxi was "bothering" us.

Me – Where do you want to go, Shirley?

Shirley – Shop

Shirley's brevity with her use of words bordered on comical and these one-word sentences with no detail whatsoever were her speciality.

Me – And which shop would that be, Shirley? Spar or Keystore? Co-op, maybe?

Shirley – Keystore. Sorry, John

Me – No problem, Shirley

I pulled away once I'd ensured Shirley's seatbelt was secured and engaged in my usual meaningless patter to fill the void.

Me – I think it might rain later

Shirley – Oh I hope not

Me – Oh why is that, Shirley? You off somewhere later? Gardening, maybe?

Shirley – No. Stay in and watch telly

This little exchange happened around ninety percent of her hires when she went to one of Dalmellington's three wee grocery shops. The other ten percent of the time she went to the bank. She always just watched television and never went anywhere except maybe to her brother's house, and then watched the telly at his place. She never caused anyone any bother though, unlike some people, and I liked her. I pulled up outside the Keystore.

Shirley – Can you wait here for me, John? I only need milk

Me – Sure. I'll see you back here in a minute

Shirley darted erratically into the Keystore with her eyes scanning everywhere like she was under sniper fire. Before I even got chance to fire up Gem Drop on my phone, she was back in the taxi like she'd just pulled a caper at the bank, which is situated directly opposite. I caught sight of a huge pack of kitchen roll in her bag but no milk. Maybe the milk is hidden from view, and it was none of my business anyway.

Me – All done, Shirley?

Shirley – Aye

Me – Home then?

Shirley – Aye

I took her home with little chit-chat and she offered me a wedge of notes and a pile of change which I had to rummage through to pick out the right money. I never took a tip off her in all the hundreds of occasions I picked her up because I didn't think it was right to just help myself to an extra few coins. If I didn't get a tip off someone it honestly never bothered me, but most did tip me, and some were more than generous. I was therefore done and pootled back to base for a microwaved coffee. The taxi phone rang a wee bit later and I could see it was Shirley again and I was promptly back outside her house once more. She got in after her dash down the short driveway and we had the same chat as before with even the same destination of Keystore. Shirley told me she needed a bottle of milk again.

Me – Didn't you get milk last time, Shirley?

Shirley – No. I forgot

Me – Oh

What else can you say? I waited for her and she ran out the shop after what seemed like less than a minute and got back in the cab. I did see a bottle of milk in her bag on this occasion, otherwise I would have mentioned it to her.

Shirley – Sorry I was so long, John

Me – Not a problem, Shirley. I'm pretty quiet today

Shirley told me she just wanted to go home again, so I pulled off and we arrived at the end of Main Street where it meets the A713. There was a car approaching so I waited before I could pull out and turn left. A quiet wee village like Dalmellington sees little traffic, and I could drive from one end of the village to the other without having to wait for a single car on most of my journeys. The three number 52 buses an hour and the very occasional wood lorry servicing one of the many local forestry places which surround the village was about as busy as things got. The nearby open-cast coal mine gave us very little traffic and there was a guy who operated a few articulated lorries but I can't recall seeing them very often. They were usually well outside the village most of the time. Most traffic in the village was myself or Boss or one of Andy's drivers.

Shirley (looking at the solitary car coming) – It's awfully busy here today, John

Me – Have you ever been to London or Glasgow, Shirley?

Shirley – No. Only been to Ayr on the 52 bus

Me – I've been to London and Glasgow and most of the big cities in Britain and they're very busy places

Shirley (incredulous) – Even busier than Dalmellington?

Me – Yes. Even busier than bustling Dalmellington

I took her home and returned once more to microwaved coffee, cigarettes, chewing gum, hastily obtained snacks from either the village café or the Pit Stop, and the normal tedium of taxi driving. Shirley phoned again after an hour or so had elapsed.

She explained that she needed to go to the bank, directly opposite the Keystore, so I pootled to her house once more and within a few minutes was parked in exactly the same spot as the two previous hires with her. On the brief journey, we had little conversation, but she did show me, for some reason I didn't understand, the wedge of notes she wanted to pay in. I tried to cram in a wee bit of Gem Drop thinking the bank would have a queue, but as usual, Shirley was back out the bank in record time and I took her home through the bustling streets of the village.

An hour later she called again. Like a very bad pressing of a vinyl record, we had the same conversations as before, although this time she showed me a cheque she needed to pay in the bank, as well as yet another call at the Keystore. She promptly completed the banking and shopping in world record time, only this time I had no idea what shopping she went for because she didn't mention it. Within five minutes I took her home and incredibly, a short while later she was back on the phone again. So once more I went and picked her up after she explained to me she needed to go to the bus terminus in the square to meet a friend getting off the bus from Ayr. After picking her up for the fifth time that day, I pulled up by the terminus and extracted the required fare from the huge pile of coins she offered me.

Me – Shirley. You've been in the taxi a lot today, and I reckon you could have done all your shopping and banking and stuff in just one or two trips. Save a fortune in money, you would

Shirley – Ooh I never thought, John

Needless to say that she continued to use our services without an ounce of planning or forethought whatsoever, although I never had her in the taxi five times in one day again.

Faeces

Glasgow Queen Street railway station was where Boss sent me on a cold February evening to pick up a young lad who had used our taxis a few times according to Boss, although I'd never met him myself. He was getting off the train from Aberdeen and I was to collect him and take him to Maybole. I made a sign with the lad's name on it to wave at anyone fitting Boss's vague description of him, which was a regular looking guy of nineteen years, leaving a certain platform at the appropriate time. I also had to park the taxi somewhere, but I found a good spot thanks to Boss's great guidance and selected a good vantage point to stand like a silly sausage with my flimsy piece of cardboard.

The arrivals board told me the Aberdeen train had arrived so I stood firm and hoped he would spot me. He found me within a few minutes and we headed out for where I'd parked up. Safely inside the car, with the lad opting for the back seat, I soon navigated my way towards the M8 through Glasgow's grid-like streets, which I always found fairly easy to negotiate. The M8 motorway which winds its way through the city was a bit of a fairground ride in comparison. The lad hardly said a word once the initial greetings were out the way and he complained his stomach ached while moaning and groaning the entire time. I concentrated on driving, and once I was off the M8 and on the M77 towards Ayr I felt much better and relaxed.

The windows were up and the heater was on, so when I caught a whiff of what I assumed to be a cloud of anal wind, it was quite intense. I eased both front windows down an inch, and then another.

Lad – Sorry about that, driver, but my guts are killing me

Me – No worries, mate. I've been known to do the occasional bottom burp

I had a wee chuckle I must admit. We neared Kilmarnock but the smell of that bottom burp lingered and I wondered what had the guy eaten to create such an awful pong that hung around so much. I wound the windows down a wee bit more and ploughed on towards Ayr once Kilmarnock was passed.

Lad – Driver, it's a wee bit cold in here now with those windows down. Can you wind them back up, please?

Me – Sure

I wound the windows back up but the stench quickly became unbearable once more. "What had this guy eaten," I wondered.

Lad – Oh dear

Me – Another fart? Ah, no worries

Lad – Driver. I've not done a fart. I've done an actual jobbie

Me – Err... You are joking, I hope

Lad – I'm not joking driver. The first one was a fart... I think, but that last one definitely wasn't. Sorry about this but my guts just let go

Me – Bloody hell

We approached Ayr, and I needed to get the lad to Maybole no matter how bad the car stunk or what state it was in. He was clearly very ill, not a drunken herbert otherwise I'd have turfed him out the car there and then. Thankfully the traffic was light as we skirted Prestwick and pressed on down what was now the A77.

Me – You keep your trousers on, pal. I'll get you home as soon as I can, but let's be realistic about this. Some of that shit will seep through your trousers onto the car seat, so the less you move about the better

Lad – Aye

As soon as I stopped outside his house, he phoned his mother and she came out, paid me extra for the inconvenience and soilage and I drove away pulling into a lay-by on the way back to the office. I took a quick look at what he'd left behind, which wasn't too bad considering what had happened. It could have been a whole lot worse. With all the windows wound fully down after a quick phone call to Boss, I drove back to Dalmellington with my head half out the window like a dog. The next day, Boss got the car cleaned out thoroughly and he even had a phone call from the lad expressing his profuse apologies. Another incident that was thankfully never repeated.

Brownhills

Getting folks messages was a task I performed for a number of regulars over the years. From a few items up to a week's worth of shopping, I would often get a call to pop round the Co-op, Keystore or Spar for someone. Doug was one such user of this service we offered sparingly to people we knew well, and he appreciated it very much. He had difficulty walking and we often chatted about this and that, and I grew quite fond of the guy. He was a nice, decent bloke, around fifty years of age, and it was a pleasure to get his messages two or three times a week depending on when he phoned us up. Boss or myself would pick his shopping list up when we passed his house, get the items, and drop them round to him when we next passed by. He would never be in desperate need for anything, but if he was, we'd get his messages back to him as soon as we could. A nice and easy relaxed arrangement that suited both parties fine.

Doug and I would chat occasionally if I had the phone and wasn't particularly busy. One day he asked me about my accent so I told him I was born in Birmingham and had spent most of my formative years living in that area. He put on a bad Brummie accent and told me he used to work in Brownhills, which is a town just to the north of Birmingham, and he also mentioned a job he did at the National Exhibition Centre just to the east.

Boss did Doug's shopping run one Friday just after this

brief chat, and when I went in to work the next day he handed me a big photo album.

Boss – Doug said this is for you to look at

Me – I wonder why Doug wants me to look at these? I don't remember chatting about photos and stuff. I just told him I was from Birmingham and he said he'd worked in nearby Brownhills and the NEC

Boss – Well, have a look so that when you drop it back to him, you'll ken what the photos are about because he'll ask what you think of them

Me – Aye I will

Boss and myself had a brief look at the photos and they were all snaps of Doug fishing and hiking and camping and such like when he was a younger man before he fell ill. Some of the pictures had his dog and his two sons in and most of them were pretty good photos to be fair. They didn't have fingers over the lens and trees appearing to grow out of people's heads and all the usual mistakes you might expect. All of them were taken in the Dalmellington area, and Boss could actually name nearly every brae and loch on the photos too.

I stuck the photo album in the boot of the taxi, after I'd had a good look at them, and went about my day. Doug phoned up a few days later, and I drove over shortly afterwards to collect his shopping list.

Me – Hi, Doug. Here's your photo album. Some nice photos in there

Doug – Aye. When I was a wee bit younger

Me – Good photography too. Lighting and angles and all that pish

Doug – Aye thanks, John. Well, you're from Brownhills, aren't you? You'll ken these places

Me – Eh?

Doug – In the photos. You'll ken the places in the photos

Me – What places? Weren't they all taken around here?

Doug – Well some were, but some are down in Brownhills

Me – Really? I couldn't see any Brownhills photos, Doug. Just you and your two lads with your dog. Camping and fishing and all that stuff

Doug (in a bad Brummie accent) – Aye. In Brownhills

Me – Oh. Well I didn't know Brownhills had lochs and forest and all that, Doug

Doug – No worries, John

I was now a wee bit confused as to what Doug was on about, but all the same, I got his shopping done and later that morning I popped into the Pit Stop and chatted with Paula behind the counter.

Paula – What's wrong, John? You look bothered

Me – I've just been chatting with one of my regulars and I'm totally confused by what they were telling me. Nothing important really

Paula – Go on, tell me. I'm all ears

Me – Well, you know I'm from Birmingham

Paula (laughing) – I did suspect there was something wrong with you but carry on

Me – My regular mentioned Brownhills near Birmingham but I've never been there. So, he showed me some photos which he says are of Brownhills

Paula – Yes. And?

Me – All the photos are local to here. Lochs and hills and forests and stuff. Brownhills is a wee place near Birmingham

Paula – Oh he's talking about the Brownhills down the road here. Near Carsphairn

Me – But he mentioned Birmingham and working at the NEC

Paula – He must mean the one just down the road. Not all the way down near Birmingham

Me – Then why does he keep putting on a bad Brummie accent whenever he talks about the place?

Paula – I've got no idea, John

Me – I'll keep you posted

Paula (laughing) – Please do

That evening I did a bit of research into any area called Brownhills I could find, and even had a wee look at Brownhills near Birmingham on Google Street View. I found a lake near to it called Chasewater, but the entire area didn't have much in the way of forests and hills, unlike Dalmellington. I found no mention of the local Brownhills just down the road and assumed it must be a local name rather than an official one. In any case there appeared to be just two Brownhills in the whole of Britain and they're about three hundred miles apart. The next time I called in at Doug's to pick up his messages list, we had a wee chat.

Me – Hi, Doug

Doug (handing me his list) – Hi, John. Here's my wee list. The usual stuff

Me – OK, Doug. I'll get this lot back to you soon. Hey, I had a look at Brownhills on the internet the other day. Seems like a nice enough place

Doug – Ooh it's great, John

Me – Doug, I'm a bit confused about these Brownhills places

Doug – How do you mean?

Me – Well, you know I'm from Birmingham

Doug (in a bad Brummie accent) – Aye Birmingham

Me – There's a Brownhills near there

Doug – Aye Brownhills. It's a great place

Me – Is there a Brownhills down the road here?

Doug – Aye, just down the road about ten miles

Me – Near Carsphairn?

Doug – Aye

Me – Not near Birmingham?

Doug (again in his bad accent) – Birmingham

I honestly hadn't got a clue what Doug was on about so I cut the conversation short, made my excuses and left to get his shopping. A short while later I dropped his messages off and made another speedy exit because I was actually quite busy.

A few days slipped quietly by, and I was sat in the office playing my beloved Gem Drop one afternoon when Doug called, which I thought unusual because he normally phoned around 10am.

Me – Hi, Doug. What can I do for you?

Doug – Hi, John. I'm watching the telly

Me – Anything good on?

Doug – Yes. I'm watching a game show

Me – Nice

Doug – Aye there's a woman on it from down your way

Me – Birmingham?

Doug – Aye she's from Brownhills

Me – Oh really

Doug – You're from Brownhills, aren't you, John?

Me – No Doug. I'm from Birmingham

Doug – Oh. But you ken Brownhills, don't you?

Me – Not really Doug. I know where it is... Well, I think I do

Doug – Well, this woman on the telly is from there

Me – Let's hope she wins

Doug (in his bad Brummie accent) – Aye. Birmingham

That was the end of the conversation. The frustrating thing for me was that shortly after the Brownhills episode I finished taxi driving so I never did manage to get to the bottom of what, for me, was a very confused situation. Was Doug confusing the two Brownhills? No way could he think they were the same place, but it seemed to be both the only possible and impossible answer at the same time. I never got to find out and it will forever remain a mystery to me.

PART THREE – MOTORCYCLE STORIES

Czech Republic[1] Motorcycling Holiday 1993

A lot of my friends have heard bits of this yarn over the years and once they found out I was writing a second book of taxi stories, they said that this motorcycle tale is so good it should be included too... like a bonus track on a CD or something. Anyway, I hope you enjoy it.

I met Sophie in May 1993. She was a quietly spoken lady but since we shared a love of heavy metal music we soon got along and started dating. We saw a lot of each other over the following weeks and soon became inseparable. The summer of that year arrived and I asked if she fancied a motorcycle holiday to the Czech Republic along with a friend of mine, Gary. He knew someone with a flat in Prague that we could rent cheaply

---

1   At the time of writing this story in 2017/18, the Czech Republic's English name has been changed to 'Czechia', but I have decided to use the name in place at the time the events occurred.

for a few days and we could go to the Czech Motorcycle Grand Prix at Brno too. I told her I'd been on numerous jaunts around various European countries such as France, Italy, Switzerland and Germany over the years and she'd have nothing to worry about. She liked the sound of it, so I planned everything out with my usual precision for such a journey including spare parts for the bike and a good map of Europe, and the Czech Republic specifically.

Sophie had never been on a motorcycle at all never mind a jaunt around Europe so we embarked on a few weekends away in Wales to acclimatise her to long distances on two wheels. Truth be told she handled long journeys better than I did. I would often complain of an aching bottom or stiff shoulders and she would always look like a million dollars without a care in the world. I had previously ridden to the south of France three times and a ride to the Italian lakes via Switzerland on another occasion and four trips to the 24 hour Le Mans races in the 1980s and I always ached through each of them. I always needed a few days doing nothing at all when I returned home to recover from my various European jaunts.

Gary, who incidentally looks a bit like the children's television puppet character Captain Scarlet, was a guy I had known since we left school many years previously and he would be travelling on his Kawasaki GPZ. Sophie and I would be on my Yamaha XJ which I had owned for about eight years at this point. This was in the days before widespread mobile phone and internet use so consequently none of us had a mobile phone and booking the ferry was a paper booking form and cheque in the post task. With the ferry arranged, passports, various currencies and travellers' cheques tucked away and panniers stuffed with everything you could cram in, we were off. Until we got to Oxford and Gary promptly came off his bike at a roundabout on the outskirts of the city where the A44 meets the A40. We discovered a large patch of diesel fuel, which had been slopped there presumably from an overfilled tank on a truck or bus. The damage to Gary's bike amounted to a broken indicator lens and some scuffed panniers. Apart from pride, Gary suffered no injury at all from the low-speed incident. We had opted to avoid the M40 from Birmingham because we were on holiday and preferred a more scenic route but I think Gary regretted that decision.

We pressed on, skirted London, soon arrived in Dover and caught the ferry to Calais. A calm voyage led to us alighting in France late in the day. In a few hours it would be dark but we had the idea of riding through Belgium as quickly as we could to Germany and finding a cheap hotel there rather than finding a place now. Why we did this I have no idea. It wasn't as if we had to get to Prague in record time.

The Grand Prix was on 22 August and we rode out on 14 August, giving us plenty of time, but I had the impression that Gary wanted to get a move on and get to the flat in Prague by the end of the next day. Sophie and myself had the idea of pottering through Germany over a period of a few days doing a bit of tourism on the way, but we couldn't lose Gary as he swept through the darkening motorways of Belgium towards the German border because, and this is very important, *only he knew where we were going,* and he had an address scrawled on a piece of paper. All I had was Gary's tail light to follow as the skies finally hit total darkness apart from the light of other vehicles and street lights.

I think it was the Belgian city of Liege where it all went wrong. It was now very late indeed and, as well as being stiff and tired, I was worried about finding a hotel at this hour. I kept up with Gary's GPZ easily enough, but we soon hit some roadworks which were poorly marked out and a gap formed between us... then I lost sight of him... then suddenly the roadworks cleared and although I caned the Yamaha to catch up with where I thought Gary would be, I never came across him. I pulled into a Belgian motorway services and crawled around the complex looking for a lime-green Kawasaki. Gary wasn't there which left Sophie and myself not knowing where we were headed, except to Prague, which is a very vague address indeed.

Sophie – What do we do now?

Me – Get off this motorway and find a hotel at the next town

Sophie – I thought you said these motorcycle holidays were fun?

Me – Yeah well...

We both laughed because there was nothing else we could do and climbed back on the Yamaha, got off the motorway at Eupen, rode down an almost dead straight main road for many miles, and eventually reached the German border near Monschau. We soon came across a small hotel with a stack of motorcycles parked outside. None of them was a British-registered lime-green Kawasaki, which was a long shot but it did cross my mind. I pulled up hoping they had a room available. Sophie spoke a bit of German so she went in and after a few minutes emerged with a big smile on her face. We had the last room available, so a bit of luck had come our way and we went to bed exhausted. The hotel owner had let me put the Yamaha in his garage, too.

Hotel in Monschau, Germany

Despite the noise of the party that all the local bikers were enjoying at the hotel, Sophie and I promptly fell asleep. I thought someone came into the room at one point and I half woke up, but I dismissed it as a vivid dream. After a much-needed and very deep sleep, we woke the next morning to a hearty German breakfast followed by a revised plan for the remainder of our holiday. We would continue on our way to Prague but would take our time and visit some sights along the way rather than blasting through Germany in one day, which is what Gary was probably planning to do. We would surely never find him now, so we opted to head for the flat we didn't know the address of at a leisurely pace, and if we couldn't find Gary in Prague, which I was sure we wouldn't, we would stay in a hotel and head for the Grand Prix in Brno in our own time. I made a comment to Sophie that there couldn't be many lime-green GPZ 900s in the Czech Republic so we'd find him easily enough but I don't think she took me seriously.

That morning we set off on our journey to mystery and soon ended up in the city of Mannheim where we stopped for coffee and a bite to eat. There was a park nearby so we relaxed and watched some locals playing a game of chess on one of those large outdoor sets. A huge billboard caught my eye as we strolled back to the bike and I asked Sophie what it said.

Sophie – Ooh something about traffic accidents... let's all be safe and take care... that kind of stuff

We got back on the Yamaha and I pulled away into the busy city traffic as we headed for Schwabisch Hall, which we had selected as the destination for that day. We would stay there a day or so before heading on to Nuremberg then the Czech Republic. I rode past a side street with cars merging from the right and out the corner of my right eye I caught sight of a car hurtling in our direction. Whump! A huge crashing noise filled the air, but we were still upright on the Yamaha. The car had ploughed directly into the car immediately behind us, moments after reading a sign about road safety too. I quickly decided I would be of no assistance whatsoever to anyone in the crash and that I had nothing to do with it anyway so I carried on. Sophie leaned forward and shouted in my ear. Communication on a motorcycle is not very easy with a crash helmet on.

Sophie – What was that noise?

Me (I took another look in my mirror) – Oh I think the car behind us just blew up. I can see smoke coming out the engine. People gathering around it now

I pressed on and we soon arrived at the very nice German town of Schwabisch Hall where we stayed for a couple of days. It was here I explained to Sophie about the accident behind us. Gary coming off, getting split from him and then having such a close shave. This holiday was going to be a classic and this was only the first full day of it. A pleasant day there followed by a one-day stopover in Nuremberg and we then headed for the Czech Republic itself. We crossed the border and quickly came to the small town of Cheb where I grabbed some Czech currency at a local bank then we continued on to Karlovy Vary where we decided to stop for that particular night.

On the way to Karlovy Vary, a bee or some such insect somehow managed to sting me in my scrotum through my leather jeans. I was in a great deal of pain and was involuntarily trying to clamp my legs together which is impossible on a motorcycle, but fortunately, a small lay-by came into view so I quickly swung into it and stopped sharply.

Me – Bloody hell!

Sophie – What's wrong?

Me – Something has stung me in my balls

I whipped my gloves and helmet off and pulled my leather jeans down. I couldn't see anything but was in great pain.

Me – Sophie, you got to help me sweetie. Please

Sophie – Jeez!

Sophie swung into action and I can only imagine the view that passing motorists were getting of a half-naked man stood by his motorcycle with a leather-clad lady examining his genitalia.

Sophie – Got it!

Me – Oh, Sophie. You darling

Sophie – Bloody hell it was a big one

Me – Well thanks, sweetie, but I don't like to brag about it

We were soon on our way and after a short while, I stopped at another lay-by for a much-needed spot of lunch. I opted for what looked like a burger from the greasy roadside food van but it didn't taste very nice so most of it ended up in a bin. Sophie settled for just a coffee which was passable, and we hit the road once again shortly arriving in Karlovy Vary. I scooted around for a while and we ended up in a car park where I spotted a tourist information notice board. I ambled over to it and couldn't read any of it, so I walked back to Sophie and the bike. A man approached me carrying a tatty cardboard folder in his hand. For some reason I had the notion he was a parking official who was going to book me for some trivial parking offence, then I realised I wasn't in the UK anymore.

Man – You British?

Me – Yes, we are

Man – You want a place to stay?

Me – Yes. You know a good hotel?

Man – I know a good private house. Very cheap

He showed us some pictures from the folder he had with him. It was a home-made brochure and it had English and German writing in it as well as Czech. It looked a decent sort of place so Sophie and I had a very brief chat and we decided to go and take a look. The man climbed into a beat-up little Yugo car and we followed him a few miles to the outskirts of the city where we ended up in a very nice-looking part of town and he stopped outside a decent looking detached house. Sophie and I climbed off the bike. The man went and opened the front door and beckoned us to come with him.

Me – Looks OK so far, Sophie

Sophie – It does

Me – I don't think this guy has brought us here to murder us either. Seems legitimate to me. A guy trying to make a living a few years after the fall of communism. The Czech Republic only formed this year, too. What do you think?

Sophie – Let's have a look inside

We followed the man into the house and a quick look round revealed a very nice place with all the usual facilities, and even though the décor was somewhat dated it was very homely. As a bonus, the house a few doors along was a restaurant so we agreed on a deal which was an absolute bargain. He wanted paying in US dollars so we went back to the centre of Karlovy Vary where I exchanged some travellers' cheques for the required amount of dollars. This created some stern questions from the lady behind the counter until a colleague waved her protests away.

We then followed the man back to the house, paid him and got the keys. All this while, and despite the pain in my scrotum easing considerably, my stomach had been rumbling and groaning and I felt a wee bit poorly. I thought it was probably the bee sting or maybe even the inedible burger. Either way, Sophie and myself were soon relaxing on the balcony which had a jolly nice view of the surrounding countryside, still in our motorcycle leathers and boots, listening to the only record that the stereo system had with it; Duran Duran's *Rio* album. Sophie and myself would have preferred something heavier but it took our minds off the recent goings-on. Even so, after a while my stomach was hurting even more and I went to the toilet. I pulled down my leather jeans and while I was bent over, my bottom let go with the most awful explosion of diarrhoea I had ever known. I flopped back onto the toilet and noticed the mess everywhere. The stench was unbearable.

Me – Bloody hell!

Sophie (through the door) – What's up?

Me – Sophie, I've been very ill everywhere with my bottom. It's all brown and smelly in here

Sophie – Bloody hell, John!

Me – Sorry, sweetie

Sophie – How bad is it in there?

Me (looking at the mess around me) – Pretty bad, Sophie. Mop-and-bucket job, I think. I feel terrible

Sophie – I'll go and find some stuff to clean up

Sophie went off and I sat there for a while sweating profusely amid the stench and awful mess on the floor. Luckily it was a tiled floor so it should clean up nicely. I cleaned myself as best I could, then opened a window and stripped off my leather jeans and motorcycle boots and cleaned them in the bath. Sophie soon returned and voluntarily mopped up the mess I had made while I took an urgently needed shower.

Sophie – Must have been that burger you ate at that grotty lay-by

Me – Or the bee sting. They can upset your insides, I imagine

Sophie – Are all your motorcycle holidays like this? Accidents, losing your best friend, nearly getting hit ourselves, exposing your genitals at the side of the main road and shitting everywhere?

Me – Err... Sophie, you make it sound so negative, sweetie. This is the first time all those five things have happened. Really...

The mess was soon cleaned up and after a few hours lay down on the sofa I felt better and we had a very enjoyable meal at the house a few doors away. The following morning, I felt better still, which surprised me. We were preparing to stay there for another day or so but we decided to move on to Prague and try to find the flat we didn't know the address of. We left the house sparkling clean and I dropped the keys back through the letterbox as instructed, then after a brief and thankfully uneventful ride, we approached the outskirts of Prague. I had no idea where I was going and had no plan whatsoever except to maybe spot Gary's Kawasaki somewhere as we rode along. My real plan was to get a map of the city and find a good hotel where Sophie and myself would stay for three or four days over the weekend spanning the Grand Prix in Brno, which is about one hundred and twenty miles to the south-east.

Tourist Information Kiosk, Prague

I saw a small tourist information kiosk at the side of the road just as we crossed over the Prague city limits and buildings began to appear, and decided to stop there for a map and maybe some advice towards a good hotel. Sophie stayed outside while I entered the tiny building and met a man stood behind a small table covered in maps and leaflets.

Me – Hello

Kiosk Man (in impeccable English) – Hello, Sir. How may I help you?

Me – I need a street map of Prague, please. I'm trying to find a place

Kiosk Man – What sort of place, Sir? A hotel, maybe?

Me – It might come to that. I lost my friend back in Belgium. We got split up. He knows the address of the place we were heading for but I don't, so me and my girlfriend are in a difficult situation now

Kiosk Man reached into a pocket, pulled out a piece of paper and looked at it.

Kiosk Man – Is your name John?

Me (very surprised) – Err... yes, it is

Kiosk Man – Your friend Gary was here yesterday on his Kawasaki. He asked me to give you this

The man handed me a piece of paper with an address written

on it. I simply could not believe what was happening, and while I slowly shook my head I stepped outside and told Sophie whereupon she nearly collapsed on the ground. I went back inside the kiosk and the man had unfolded a street map of Prague on the table. He pointed at a spot and marked it in pencil.

Kiosk Man – The address you need to go is here

I couldn't thank the guy enough. This amazing state of affairs cheered Sophie and myself up enormously, and we climbed back on the Yamaha knowing we would soon be reunited with our friend. Gary had obviously stopped at the very same kiosk the day before and had an inkling that I would do the very same thing. The chances of this happening must have been astronomical. I folded the map up and secured it in my tank bag top for ease of referral while I rode to the street that Kiosk Man had highlighted. We soon arrived at a jolly nice detached house in a sleepy suburb which had no sign of life and no lime-green Kawasaki either. We decided to just hang about and wait until Gary returned from where we assumed he must have gone. Sophie and I spent a good while loafing about and chatting about the events of the past few days until eventually a man approached us from next door.

Neighbour – Hello

Me – Hello. I'm John and this is my girlfriend Sophie. We're from England looking for my friend, Gary. Maybe you've seen him? He is on a lime-green Kawasaki

Sophie – Hello

Neighbour – Your friend was here yesterday on his motorcycle and then went off again. I haven't seen him since. I didn't speak with him

Me – Oh that's a pity. We got split up in Belgium and only he knows the flat we are staying at in Prague

Neighbour – The man who lives here owns some flats in a district called Zizkov. He must have sent your friend there. There are numerous tower blocks there and he owns a few flats. He has gone away on business for a few days now. Show me your map, please

The neighbour pointed to the map secured on my petrol tank, which I then removed so we could refer to it easier. He highlighted what appeared to be a large sprawl of tower blocks spanning quite a large area over many streets.

Neighbour – I don't know which block I'm afraid. He's my neighbour and all I know is that he owns some properties in that area. Your friend must be there

Me – We'll find him easily enough, my friend. Thank you very much

Sophie – Thank you. This is incredible, John

Me – Meh... not really, after everything else that's happened

Sophie and I remounted my 900 and we headed off on yet another leg of the strangest holiday I had ever known and would probably ever have again, although it wasn't a holiday anymore; It was more like a kind of epic game of hide-and-seek or a new television show. Sophie was an excellent map reader and navigator, so she held the map and shouted occasional instructions as I pootled through the centre of Prague headed for Zizkov. It was a pity that the neighbour didn't know the exact block or address, but aside from that; why did Kiosk Man send us to that house rather than the flat in Zizkov? Didn't Gary tell Kiosk Man where the tower block in Zizkov was? None of it made much sense but one thing was for sure; I would never forget any of this.

We soon arrived in Zizkov and came across a huge sprawling complex of grim and sad looking tower blocks. Only the varying shades of grey differentiated them from each other. It was mid-afternoon yet there were hardly any people about, and with only the occasional car parked up in the virtually empty car park areas, the entire district looked half abandoned. One or two roadside kiosks and mobile shops were set up here and there too. I crawled round and round the huge estate not having any idea what to do or where to go.

The only plan I had, and the only plan that would work now, was to actually come across Gary's hideous lime-green Kawasaki GPZ 900 parked up at the entrance to one of the many tower blocks I was now slowly riding past. Sophie and myself took a side of the road each scanning for clues as I rode along seeing nothing other than grey tower block after yet another grey tower block. I estimated every one of them to be about ten floors each and all built in the same period too. Everything looked the same. I also half expected someone to run over to us and ask if we knew Gary and give us yet another address to find.

Suddenly into view appeared Gary's GPZ parked up at the doorway to one of the towers. The relief was incredible. Sophie bounced up and down on the seat as I briskly swept up the entrance road to the block, revved the engine up, tooted my horn a few times then switched the bike off. I looked at the huge panel of buttons near the door but obviously had no idea which one to press. It would be a case of pressing every one until Gary answered I decided. I then looked up the sheer wall of drab concrete and noticed that most of the windows in each flat were open due to it being a very hot August day.

Me (at the top of my voice) – Garyyyyy!!!!

A few heads appeared out of some windows, then the face of my oldest and best friend appeared from about the fifth floor.

Gary (laughing) – You took your time!

Me – Found you!

I locked the bike up and Sophie and myself were soon inside after Gary came down to let us in. The flat was pretty cool to be honest, and we soon settled in and relaxed like never before.

Me – Gary, why didn't you give the guy in the tourist info kiosk the address of this place? Why did we have to go to the other house first?

Gary – Aha! Well, I only had the address of that house where the owner lives. He sent me on here and I just assumed he'd send you here himself once you got to his house. He said that giving me the address of this flat in the first place would have been pointless because it's so hard to find in this maze of concrete, so he gave me a detailed map and explanation when I got to his house

Me – He wasn't in but his neighbour sent us here

Gary – Yeah well it all worked out in the end. Good job I guessed you'd stop at that first kiosk. I know how your mind works, mate

Sophie (shaking her head) – Un-be-lievable

After a few days of sightseeing and relaxing we all set off on the one-hundred-and-twenty-mile jaunt to Brno to take in the 1993 Czech Motorcycle Grand Prix which was the 11th round of the 14-round season. Both Sophie and myself would be rooting for Wayne Rainey riding for Yamaha who had won the previous three 500cc World Championships from 1990 to 1992 and was the current leader of the 1993 500cc Grand Prix season with just four rounds to go. We both liked the guy and... well, he rode a Yamaha like I did, so that was as good a reason as any.

The race was as hot and sticky and noisy as can be expected, and between bends four and five the three of us had a great view of Rainey winning the race and extending his lead in the championship to eleven points with three rounds left.

We could have had no idea of the tragedy that befell Wayne

at the next Grand Prix round in Italy two weeks after his Brno victory when his spine was broken in an awful accident that stunned the entire world of motorcycle racing. One of the best riders who ever lived would never ride or race or even walk again. He was paralysed from the chest down and the tragic news hit me and everyone else very hard. I saw him win his last race after I'd had what I considered to be a difficult few days. Those trivial incidents of mine paled into total insignificance and made me realise how lucky I was and how cruel life can sometimes turn out.

The remainder of our holiday passed relatively event-free compared to the first week, and we returned home back to our more normal lives. Meeting up with Gary shortly after we'd all returned, we naturally talked about the events of the holiday in more detail, particularly what happened after we got split from each other in Belgium. It turned out that the headlight on his bike stopped working so he pulled over to fix it.

Gary – My headlight went out so I pulled onto the shoulder to repair it. It was dark and difficult so it took me some time. Eventually, I got it sorted and left the motorway at Eupen...

Me – I pulled off the motorway at Eupen, too

Gary – I didn't know where you were, but I saw some motorcycles go past me while I was fixing my bike, so you could have been one of them. Anyway, I rode through Eupen and then headed for Germany along a straight road through a heavily wooded area

Me – Yeah me too. I saw a huge stag on the side of that road. Quite scary when all of a sudden it appeared into view with my headlight

Gary – I arrived at the next big town after that and pulled into a hotel with a lot of motorcycles parked outside

Me – You are joking

Gary – No

Me – That must be the hotel Sophie and I stopped at

Gary – I couldn't see your bike

Me – The owner let me put my bike in the garage

Gary – Wow. Anyway, the guy at the hotel showed me to a room but there was someone there asleep in bed. So funny. I don't think he knew there was anyone in the room but we left them alone. He had no other rooms so he sent me to a place up the road and I stayed there

Sophie – John, didn't you say to me that you thought someone came in the room when we were in bed?

Me – Yes, I remember now! I thought it was a dream or something. I bet that was you Gary

Gary – You must have ridden past me while I was fixing my

bike, got to that hotel first then I rolled up a while later. It must have been a different guy showing me the room to the guy who saw you two

Sophie – Un-be-lievable times ten

The amazing coincidences and bizarre events of that holiday will live with us forever and is a source of great amusement even now. No holiday I've had since then or will have in the future will ever come close to it.

Over the following few years, Sophie and myself enjoyed many more European jaunts on my trusty Yamaha and in all those subsequent holidays we never had a week remotely close to that first week of the Czech Republic trip. We went to Denmark on three different holidays and Hungary and Austria on another occasion, and those trips went much smoother for us in comparison.

The only incidents of note occurred in Hungary where Sophie did the usual routine we had established over many years where she would go and check out the bed and breakfast or hotel room, while I sat on the bike staring into space relaxing my shoulders. Her language skills far exceeded mine, and I would have agreed to stay in any room, to be honest. She would usually emerge and give me a thumbs-up to signal the room looked decent and we were staying. However, I pulled up outside a rural place on our Hungarian trip, a country we thoroughly enjoyed otherwise, and I waited for Sophie to perform her inspection. Very shortly after she entered, instead of the more usual five minutes or so, she ran out the door putting her crash helmet on shouting "Go go go!" as she leapt on the back of the Yamaha in one bound and slapped me hard on the back. I accelerated away and after a few hundred yards leant back and shouted Sophie for an explanation.

Me – Bad, was it?

Sophie – Bad?! You bet it was. Even you would have turned it down

Me – Bad, then

Sophie – No way would I stay in a place like that. Eww!!

So that was that, but we soon found a room elsewhere. On the same Hungarian holiday, on what must have been the hottest day I can ever remember riding a motorcycle in, I pulled into a rural petrol station to fill the bike up and have a relax for five minutes. After filling the bike to the brim, I pushed it over to a grassed area and Sophie and I both sat down in some shade for a few moments. I noticed something dripping off the bottom of the bike's engine. It looked like water.

Me – We haven't been through any puddles, have we?

Sophie – It's the hottest day since time began, and it hasn't rained for ages, John. No, we haven't

Me – I thought not. I wonder what that liquid is dripping off the bike?

I went over for a closer look and soon discovered it was petrol leaking from a small hole that had formed in the bottom of the petrol tank directly above the red-hot engine.

Me – Shit!

Sophie – What is it?

Me – Petrol. Hole in the tank and I've just filled the damn thing up

Sophie – Oh dear. What are you going to do?

Me – Drain it out. I need a big container. I'll go and see the lad in the shop

The petrol station was small and there was only one young lad working there but he spoke pretty good English when I'd paid for my fuel minutes earlier. I went back into the wee shop and explained my predicament. He quickly located two empty plastic canisters that could easily hold the five gallons my tank was holding, and we fabricated a funnel out of an empty plastic bottle. We went out to the bike, had the petrol tank off within minutes and began the tiresome process of draining the fuel off into the two containers.

Petrol Guy – I know a man who can fix your tank. I will telephone him now.

Weld Man, Petrol Guy and the author draining fuel from the leaking petrol tank in Hungary

He went back in the shop and within about ten minutes a guy in a beat-up old car arrived and came straight over to the bike as I drained the last of the fuel out. He had a quick look at the small pinhole that had broken through a tiny patch of rust and nodded at me saying something in Hungarian, which Petrol Guy translated as "He can weld this for you."

Sophie – He's going to weld the tank? That sounds like it will just explode

Me – Yeah well, unless we can fix it the holiday effectively ends here at this petrol station. The only other options are to find a motorcycle breakers yard with a tank off an XJ900 lying about, which is actually possible, buy a new tank from a dealer, which is also possible, or lash a tank on from some other bike with loads of gaffer tape. If this guy can fix the tank though, we're sorted. If he blows it up then we go to a breakers yard, or dealers, or failing that we abandon the holiday.

Sophie – I guess so

Sophie stayed with the bike while I went off with Weld Man. I was trusting the guy totally, but I knew that petrol and welding don't generally mix. I had visions of an exploding petrol tank flying through the air at any minute as it exploded into pieces, then rummaging around a Hungarian breakers yard or maybe getting trailered back home with the AA. Even though I had every confidence my bike wouldn't break down, I always took out European breakdown cover. I wanted Weld Man to succeed though, and the holiday to continue.

A few miles down some back lanes we reached Weld Man's workshop and he gestured me to stay outside while he took my petrol tank inside. For the next few minutes, while I aimlessly walked up and down smoking a cigarette like an expectant father would do outside a labour ward in an old movie, I heard numerous loud pops and bangs and saw several bright flashes of light. Weld Man reappeared with a big grin on his face holding my repaired tank. The braze he had put over the pinhole was immaculate and after I thrust some money at him, which he insisted on refusing until I forced it in his pocket, he ran me back to the petrol station. With the tank back on the bike, I refilled it from the plastic containers, and within about two hours of the whole sorry saga starting, Sophie and myself were on our way once again.

Moped Racing

In the years from 1995 to 2000, some friends and I somehow got involved in what was termed 'Moped Mayhem', which was a national series of 50cc motorcycle endurance races. The circuits were situated in Anglesey, Cumbria, Lincolnshire and Yorkshire and we would race three or four times a year. The team I got together was basically a few mates and a Honda Cub four-stroke, which we ran in 1995 to 96 before we then switched to a Kawasaki AR50 two-stroke from 1997 to 2000, which I had obtained quite cheaply, together with a bunch of spare parts, tyres and various other bits and bobs in an attempt to make it go quicker. The truth was that we, actually just me, weren't very good at either making the bike competitive or riding very well ourselves, and although we never won a race, we always thoroughly enjoyed the long and hard weekends, which included either a six- or four-hour long race. Incredibly, given the 'lashed-up' nature of our wee Kawasaki, we also finished every race we entered, and actually managed a 3rd place overall in our class one particular season. The following tales all involve the Kawasaki AR50, meaning they took place between 1997 and 2000, although I can't recall which exact year.

The Accident

The 'traffic' on a one-thousand-metre-long track with about eighty mopeds on it at any one time is basically a constant stream of bikes either overtaking or being overtaken. In my case, I was overtaken by almost every bike except the much slower Class 4 bikes and some of the Class 3 machines. I held my own against some of my Class 2 counterparts but I only ever overtook the occasional bike, and that was probably due to them having a mechanical malfunction. My teammates were much better than me. I kind of just made up the numbers and ended up riding a stint only when necessary. Plus the fact it was my team. The Class 1 bikes were in a different league and I think some of those guys overtook me every lap. Basically, I was slower than most but reliable. However, it was on the very last lap of a six-hour race at Rowrah in Cumbria when I was clipped by a passing bike just before the final bend. I had caught sight of the waving chequered flag and was relieved that the final tour of the track in the quarry was nearly over. Suddenly, that relief turned to alarm as I crashed to the ground at probably thirty mph or so. Not fast, given my large bulk and the Kawasaki's poor state of tune, but tarmac hurts at any speed even with all the required leathers and body armour. I ended up sat in the middle of the track facing the direction I'd been riding. The bike came to a rest further along the baking hot tarmac and I rapidly decided I wasn't in a great position. I quickly turned my head round, saw where the rest of the bikes were that were bearing down on me racing for that chequered flag, and planned my escape route to the grass in the middle of the circuit.

That was when a bike hit me in the back. The pain was sudden and devastating, and with immense difficulty I crawled to the grassed area with the sound of screaming motorcycles all around me. The intense pain I felt in my back was insane and I finally collapsed on the grass face down... sounds filled my ears... shapes approached me... I had no idea what was happening. I rolled over onto my back, still wearing my helmet, and closed my eyes. I have no idea if I passed out or not but after an unknown period of time, I opened my eyes and could focus on things and I slowly recognised my teammates and noticed two paramedics inspecting me as they tugged off my leathers. I let out some whimpers of pain while they tried to establish the extent of the injuries. After a slow and groggy realisation of what had happened, and the paramedics' reassurance there were no serious spinal injuries, I was soon on a trip to the nearest hospital, which revealed a hairline fracture of my right shoulder blade that took about six weeks to heal up. A few inches to the left and my spine would have taken the full impact.

New Rider

Before another race meeting at Rowrah, I mentioned to Dave, a work colleague based at a different site to myself, that my team could do with another rider. We used to change riders every forty minutes and decided that three riders was the optimum number for a six- or even a four-hour long race. A forty-minute stint in the saddle would be followed by one hour and twenty minutes of 'relaxation' for each rider, while I operated the pit board and refuelling or minor repairs when needed. I could also step in and ride a stint if required like I had when I broke my shoulder blade. I told Dave that I only had two riders, Ian and Tony, for the upcoming meeting at Rowrah and he immediately decided he would like to be in the team. He rode a street motorcycle like we all did, and after a lengthy chat he was part of Pete Stewart Racing. I had named my team in honour of Tony's brother who had also raced with us and sadly passed away much too young. In a non-racing incident, I should add.

Pete Stewart Moped Endurance Racing Team. Left to right are
Ian Clarke, John Lockett, Tony Stewart and Dave

Dave lived in Berkshire, and on the weekend of the Rowrah meeting he rode the three hundred miles to the wee village of Rowrah on his Honda VFR750 and arrived halfway through Saturday's warm-up and practice sessions. The six-hour race itself was the following day. After some friendly introductions to the rest of the team, I suggested he go out for a few laps on our Kawasaki. I had already briefed him on the various rules and regulations of the racing club and he seemed very eager to get started. I thought he would be an ideal member of the team.

I was physically too big for our wee AR50 and, to be honest, not a motorcycle racer. Ian and Tony were younger and faster and weighed far less than my 110kgs. They always turned in decent performances despite our bike's imperfect set-up, and Dave would be in a similar vein we all thought.

The pit area where we were all stood overlooked the whole layout of Rowrah's thousand metre length. The track complex had been built in a disused quarry and was chiefly used as a go-kart track. Its length of one thousand metres exactly (so I understand) was required for it to qualify as a certain grade of track for national and international events. Until the extension, it came in at a much shorter length and could only be used at an amateur and local level until the necessary extra metres were added by squeezing in two extra hairpin turns in succession at the far end of the clockwise track. There were a number of bikes on the track already taking advantage of a free practice period that peppered the day-long sessions of class-specific scratch races. For at least thirty minutes we watched various bikes whizzing by and the three of us gave Dave the best advice we could before he took the Kawasaki out for the first time. The bend immediately in front and below us was the final long right-hander before the start and finish straight, which went off into the distance on our left. The exit and entry ramps, obviously in that order, were to our right, and very much like motorway ramps exited and entered at tight angles to the outside of the circuit. A race marshal with a collection of various coloured flags was stood at the top of the downward entry ramp onto the track. I pointed to him.

Me – Dave, ride over there and see Jim the marshal, he'll

inspect your leathers and helmet, then go and do a few laps. Remember: you need to virtually redline that bike in every gear to get it to move. It's not a VFR 750

Dave (laughing) – OK, John. No worries

The bike had already passed its safety inspection, but Dave would need to get Jim to pass his boots, leathers, gloves and crash helmet before being allowed on the track. Ian and Tony gave Dave some last-minute advice and hearty pats on the back, then Dave bump-started the wee two-stroke easily enough with a brief assisting push from Ian. Despite never having ridden our wee Kawasaki before, Dave seemed at home on it right from the off. He cracked the throttle a few times then pootled the long way around the paddock area, swinging the bike left and right to feel the weight and turning capabilities of it.

He soon arrived next to Jim who proceeded to inspect Dave's riding equipment before they engaged in what I knew would be a serious and fairly intense speech. Jim did not stand any nonsense whatsoever and we all knew it. I could see Jim pointing at the track and Dave nodding as he listened. Jim explained the various flags he had with him, including the black one which meant "you are out of the race" if he waved it and pointed at you or held your number aloft on a chalkboard. Jim gave Dave a thumbs-up, Dave looked over to us who all gave him a thumbs-up in return and he accelerated down the entry ramp after Jim clapped him on the back.

I looked at the track as Dave sped down the ramp and noticed the absence of bikes approaching where Dave would enter the track at that particular point. How fortunate, I thought. Dave looked over his right shoulder as he rode towards the empty track and the three of us genuinely cheered loudly... then we stopped and our mouths all opened and hands went everywhere in what seemed an eternity of confusion. Dave had braked hard, then turned sharply to the right and was riding round the circuit the WRONG WAY. We pointlessly shouted and waved our arms as he headed away from us. I looked back along the track once again, and I could see three bikes closing down on the bend Dave was approaching from the wrong direction. What do I do? What can I do?

Jim the marshal was quicker off the mark than I could have hoped or imagined. After slapping Dave on the back, he must have watched our new rider the whole way down the ramp. While we were powerless to act, Jim had sprinted down the exit ramp which Dave was swiftly nearing from the wrong side and ran onto the track frantically waving his dreaded black flag. Dave pulled to his left and onto the central grassed area (funnily enough in roughly the same spot as where I lay prostrate after my accident) and received what I imagine to be a phenomenal telling off. The clump of bikes that were travelling in the right direction zoomed past Dave who hung his head down low as the awful truth dawned on him. Jim concluded his brief lecture, turned and looked in our direction with arms outstretched as if to say, "What is your rider doing Lockett?" I held my arms outstretched as if to say, "Sorry Jim, I have absolutely no idea."

Jim black-flagged the entire practice session, and once everyone was off the track he let Dave ride up the exit ramp back to the three of us. I have never seen anyone look so dejected and embarrassed and utterly fed up as Dave did at the moment he returned to the pits. Tony took the bike off him and he stepped away a few yards before removing his crash helmet. I had assured Ian and Tony that Dave was a sensible motorcyclist I had known for a few years, despite us working at sites many miles apart, and that he knew how to ride a bike. Ian and Tony didn't question my decision at all, but all the same I could see the total bafflement bulging in their heads as Dave meekly looked at us. I had no words and neither did Dave. He was on the brink of collapsing to the ground before Ian and Tony took him by the arms and sat him down. Ian gave me a nod.

Ian – You better go see Jim

Me – Aye. Dave, I'll be back in a minute, OK mate?

Dave – Sure. OK, John. I'm so sorry mate

I went and saw Jim the head marshal and found I had no explanation whatsoever. Jim was more concerned about Dave's welfare than anything else. "No harm done," as he kindly put it. Dave never rode our Kawasaki again. He made profuse apologies to us and rode off the three hundred miles back to Berkshire. To this day I simply cannot understand how he had done what he did, and I don't think he did either. I spoke with Dave a few days after the meeting was over and he offered nothing other than apologies and not much else. I just hope he got over it quickly.

Lift to Bolton

Pete Stewart Racing had finished another weekend of thrashing our wee Kawasaki AR50 around Rowrah, which was the most used of the four circuits, and I was tiredly driving two hundred miles back home to Birmingham towing a little trailer with our bike on when I arrived at where the A66 meets the M6 at junction 40 near Penrith: the Skirsgill Interchange. Anyone who knows this junction will be aware of the complex of road maintenance buildings to the left of the slip road down to the M6 heading south. As I entered the ramp I could see a young man holding a guitar case thumbing a lift stood in the wee turn off road to the works. I had no-one else in the car with me and he looked a regular kind of chap in his twenties so I pulled over to see where he wanted to go. I'll call him Skir in this story, after the place I picked him up from.

Me – Where do you want to go, mate?

Skir – Bolton

Me – Well, that's not far out my way. Get in. Stick the guitar on the back seat

Skir opened the back door and slid his acoustic guitar case on the back seat then got in the front. As soon as he sat down he started moaning and getting on my nerves making me wish I had a time machine so I could go back a few seconds and just drive on by. I wished I'd never picked the guy up already and we were still on the slip road!

Skir – Bloody hell, mate. Your car is a mess. Look at all this rubbish all over the place.

Me – Yeah, I know, but I don't really care

My friends and I had used my car as a rubbish dump because the bin at the race circuit was too far to walk and we're lazy. The dashboard was covered in chip wrappers, burger cartons and all sorts of detritus. The floor was thick in cigarette ends and sweet wrappers and the whole car stunk of body odour and oil and general filth. The plan was to eventually clean it out when I got home. Maybe. Skir was obviously a bit repulsed by all the rubbish and voiced his revulsion in no uncertain terms. The junk irritated him and, conversely, his voice irritated me. This was going to be some journey.

After a spurt of acceleration, I merged onto the M6 south and I inwardly slapped myself about the face a few times for picking this moaning unappreciative guy up. I have picked a few hitch-hikers up over the years and had very pleasant chats with all of them. This guy was a pain in the arse already and would only get worse. Bolton couldn't arrive soon enough. It was a mild early Sunday evening with light traffic, and I tried a bit off chit-chat with the guy, who obviously liked guitars seeing as he had one with him, endeavouring to make the journey pass more agreeably and divert him from complaining about the mess. How wrong I was.

Me – What guitar you got in the case? I like guitars and music

Skir – Dunno. It's my mate's. I'm taking it back for him

That was the end of that conversation. I mentioned the beautiful sunset that was slowly enveloping us. The lakes and hills of Cumbria are a sight to behold, even from the M6, but Skir wasn't interested in anything other than continually tutting at the rubbish in my car. Eventually, he spoke about something other than the annoying levels of filth, and it came as a welcome relief.

Skir – Do you smoke?

Me – Yes, I do

Skir – Can I smoke in your car?

Me – Sure. Look at the state of it in here anyway. Coffee cups, food wrappers, sweet papers and all sorts of crap all over the place

Skir – I don't think your car should have all this mess in it

Me – I don't care, mate

Skir – What you been doing to get it so messy? There's junk everywhere

Me – Racing a motorcycle all weekend. It's on the trailer I'm towing

Skir looked back at my motorbike bobbing around on the trailer.

Skir – You win?

Me – No. I think we came sixth out of about fifteen in our class. The results take a while to confirm

Skir – Not very good

So, as well as having to sit in my untidy car, Skir was probably annoyed at sitting next to a guy who could only manage a paltry sixth place.

Me – Yeah, well, it's a laugh. We do it for fun, not to win. Winning would need lots of money and a better bike than what we have. It's a hobby for me and my mates

Skir – You smoke roll-ups?

Me – Yes, I do

Skir – I'll make you some cigarettes for giving me a lift

Me – Thanks. You don't have to, but thanks

Skir – I'll make you ten

Me – OK, ten is fine

We ploughed on down the M6 and I wished the police would stop me for a trivial offence. Or the car would break down, or aliens beam me up to their ship and go to town on me with probes, rather than endure much more of this guy. Moaning about the mess in my car. Telling me that sixth out of fifteen wasn't good in our bike race. Cheeky sod I thought he was, and I wished the next ninety miles would vanish in an instant. He picked my road atlas up off the floor, brushing away a layer of cigarette ends and sweet wrappers off it.

Skir – Can I use this as a table to roll the cigarettes on?

Me – Sure

Skir proceeded to roll cigarettes and I thought at least it would keep him quiet for a while. He placed each completed one on a flat section of dashboard then began the next. He approached the end of his cigarette-making exercise, made what he announced to be the tenth and final one, then counted them out into my left hand which he asked me to hold out.

Skir – … seven… eight… nine… fuck. I only made nine

Me – That's fine mate. Nine is good

Skir (angrily) – I promised you ten and I will make you ten. I can't believe I fucked it up. This is the problem you see. I always get stuff wrong and get into trouble. Pisses me off

Me – It's no trouble, mate. You're being more than generous making me cigarettes anyway

I just decided to agree with the guy and be as nice as possible.

Moaning about the squalid conditions in my junk heap car was one thing, but going off on one about miscounting a cigarette was the limit. He made me the tenth one while mumbling the entire time, and then plopped the road atlas back on the floor. I decided to put a tape on to fill the air with some music which may calm him down or distract him from his trivial miscalculation. I can't remember exactly what tape it was, but it would have been something like Black Sabbath or Judas Priest that soon emanated from the car's cheap stereo system. Within a few minutes, Skir announced he didn't like my music and pulled a tape out of his jacket pocket.

Skir – I don't like this music mate. Can I play this?

Me – Sure

"Cheeky sod," I thought once more. It's fair enough not liking Sabbath or Priest but we're in my car and I decide what I want to listen to. My untidy car annoyed him. My choice of music didn't agree with him. I had run out of patience with the guy miles back but I was stuck with him. It could have been anything on his tape for all I cared at this point, however. He could have put in a tape of a gearbox bearing being filled with sand, or a dustbin rolling down a hill. I just wanted what he wanted to shut him up and try, however hard, to keep him vaguely happy and not go off on one like he nearly did with the cigarette miscounting episode and to stop him harping on about the mess. He swapped the tapes over and hit play. It hissed very badly and speaking human voices rather than music came out the speakers.

Skir – Listen to that

Me – OK, what is it?

Skir – Police interview tape. My copy

"Bloody hell," I thought as I braced myself for the nonsense that would no doubt accompany it. Skir turned the volume up and I listened to what sounded like two police officers asking him questions about his whereabouts on a certain date, and were you at a certain place, and do you know a certain individual. His responses were basically "no comment" and not much else besides the occasional "yes" or "no" or a grunt of some kind. It went on for about ten minutes, although it seemed like forever. Then he asked me what I thought. Obviously, I was going to take his side even though he sounded as guilty as they come. The questions from the cops all seemed to revolve around him breaking something at his girlfriend's house, and I could easily imagine him trashing her place over something trivial.

Skir – What do you think of that? Them stupid cops asking me all those stupid questions. That ain't right, is it?

Me (acting all knowledgeable) – I think the police are technically incorrect there. I believe that asking you where you were on a certain date is what they call "entrapment"

Skir – I've heard of that. Go on

Me – The police are supposed to ask non-leading questions.

They have to be very careful how they word things otherwise whatever you say could be interpreted as one thing when in actual fact you mean something else.

The bullshit I spewed out was phenomenal. I just wanted to keep this guy sweet and be on his side until I could get him out my car. That couldn't come soon enough and we were approaching a service station in a few miles that all of a sudden I decided to stop at.

Me – I think the police were totally wrong to ask you those questions. If any of that ever got to court, I think the judge would throw the case out and the police would be in some big trouble. You'd probably get some compensation too. Ooh look, the services

I pulled into the services and parked up so I had a good clear escape route, then wearily got out the car. Skir got out as well.

Me – I need a wizz and I'm going to grab some food and drink

Skir – I'll stay here

"Damn," I thought. I was hoping he'd go to the toilet or need a drink as well. I'd make him take his guitar too, or at least leave the car so I could pop back and get out of there, but that wasn't going to happen now. I went to the toilet anyway, grabbed some snacks and a coffee then returned and we were soon back on the M6 headed for Bolton. He then asked my name and I told him it was Stewart.

Skir – I like you, Stew. You're a decent bloke

Me – Thanks. You're a decent guy, too

I don't know how but the topic of conversation thankfully drifted onto fencing panels and apparently Skir was pretty good at doing fencing and garden stuff, so if I ever needed any doing, just give him a shout. He would do me a good price and do a fantastic job too. I'd bear it in mind I told him. Then he wanted my mobile phone number and I told him I couldn't remember it, which merely led him to say that if I gave him my phone he could find the number in the menu and store it in his phone. I told him I always leave my phone in the boot so I don't get distracted while I was driving, and I just hoped that no-one would phone me in the next hour or so and it let out a hideous tune in my jacket pocket.

The daylight started to fade into a very colourful twilight, but it failed to divert me from the tedium and banality of everything Skir talked about, and his general demeanour. He brought up the cigarette miscounting episode a few times. He rambled on about the police interview tape. Fencing panels. The rubbish in my car was a continual source of irritation for him too. I had miles more of this nonsense to endure and no matter what I steered the subject to, he just droned on about utter bilge bordering on insanity. He told me why his girlfriend left him in such confusing detail I had no idea what he was talking about. I honestly didn't care, but I had to pay a modicum of attention because he kept asking me questions about the tape which he insisted on playing another time. Why oh why wasn't Bolton in Cumbria, I wished.

Eventually, before I went totally insane myself, I took the M61 exit off the M6 to Bolton and thought to myself that at least I only have about twenty more miles of this character to endure. Those tiresome miles slowly disappeared until we reached junction 5, the Bolton exit, and I was soon on the A58 for the town itself. It was dark now and never having been to Bolton before, I had no idea where I was... except near Bolton.

Me – Not far now, mate. Soon be home

Skir – Just drop me off at the end of this bit of road, Stew

Phew! The relief built rapidly inside me. I was fully expecting him to live on the other side of town and I'd have even more bothersome minutes to spend with him.

Skir – Actually, can you take this next left at the roundabout?

Me – Sure

That road led to another roundabout and I thought that surely he can't want dropping off here.

Skir – Turn right here mate and we'll be there soon

Me – OK, mate

I just wanted him out now and gone forever. We soon entered Bolton itself and I drove through quite an old part of town and approached a set of traffic lights which were turning red.

Skir – This will do, Stew. Pull in here

He pointed to a bus stop not far short of the lights, and I eased into it consciously leaving the engine running. As soon as he is out my car and those traffic lights turn green, providing the road is clear, "I am flooring the accelerator pedal," I thought. There were hardly any cars around and I reckoned a quick get-away would be easy. If he doesn't get his guitar out quick enough then tough shit. If he doesn't shut the door and it hits him then tough shit too. I had absolutely had enough of this guy. The talking rubbish didn't really bother me to be honest because I talk enough nonsense on my own; it was the veiled threat of violence and anger that got on my nerves. Yet again, he moaned about the rubbish in my car which didn't help matters either. The cheek of him!

Skir – I don't like all this rubbish in your car, Stew

Me – Don't worry about it. I'll sort it when I get...

Skir reached back into the car and grabbed handfuls of rubbish off the dashboard and scooted it all over the road, then lifted rubbish off the floor and did the same. Chip wrappers, a pizza box, burger wrappers, sweet packets and numerous old coffee cups were just strewn all over the road and that annoyed me even more. I was fuming now.

Skir – That's better

He opened the back door, grabbed his guitar case and shut the door. He then stood by the open passenger door. The traffic lights were sat on red, the engine gently idled and I left the car in first gear with my foot on the clutch. I repeatedly glanced in the mirrors checking for a vehicle that would foil my quick escape, and thankfully no-one else was about... not even pedestrians.

Skir (half leaning back in the car) – Thanks for the...

The traffic lights turned green and I dumped the clutch and floored my poor little Austin Maestro, a car not known for speedy acceleration, and it leapt forward with screeching tyres. The door slammed shut and I burst through the traffic lights in what seemed like milliseconds. A quick glance in the mirror and I saw my wee Kawasaki bobbing about quite happily on the trailer and Skir in the distance, which was the best view of him it was possible to have. I had absolutely no idea what road I was on, and I didn't care. I laughed like a drain, lit a cigarette then shortly spied a sign saying 'M61 Manchester' and I thought, "yes that will do," and headed back home in a state of total exhaustion. I felt relief and anger and a whole host of other emotions all at the same time, and arriving home later that evening was the best homecoming I'd ever known.

Epilogue

I hope you enjoyed those two motorcycle stories. With the advent of widespread mobile phone use, an incident like the Czech Republic holiday could never happen again. Nowadays, within a short while of people being split up, they could just call each other up, and send a map or something. Too easy. Smartphones have changed the taxi-driving world immensely too, and who knows what wonders the future will bring.

I sincerely wish I had more taxi tales to tell but I haven't. Google Street View is an amazing tool, and I have 'walked' around the entire village while compiling this second book to jog my memory, and that worked very nicely. In very rough mathematical terms, I estimate there to have been around one or so notable incidents per month during the four and a half years I drove a taxi, sorry, private hire vehicle, which doesn't seem that many now I've reflected on everything. The incidents seemed to never end when I was actually doing the job, but there must have been days and weeks of utter mind-numbing tedium driving up and down the same roads all day long, picking up the same people and having similar conversations almost every day. That wouldn't appear to be a great environment for stories to arise, but it was.

Incidentally, and I was absolutely amazed to discover this a few years into the job, Google's map of Dalmellington and Bellsbank had numerous roads labelled with the incorrect name. I never used Google maps to find anywhere in the villages because I had my home-made A4 laminated map, and the map in my head which formed rapidly in the first few weeks. I didn't use a satnav device either, although Boss did possess one, which Bruce sometimes used on his parcel runs. I can't remember why I searched on the internet now, but there must have been some reason or other, and I was astounded to find that a large number of Dalmellington's thirty or so roads were incorrectly named. Those twelve incorrect ones were wildly inaccurate too. They weren't labelled 'Hopes Street' instead of 'Hopes Avenue' and errors of that nature. They were so wrong it was as if they had totally mixed up Dalmellington with a completely different community altogether. I remember showing Boss, thinking that maybe they were old names similar to how many of the pubs in the village were called by an old moniker, and he creased up with laughter and vowed to never trust the internet ever again. I emailed the company responsible for Google's maps, and, whether or not it was as a direct result of my interaction with them, within a few months every street was corrected. Well, nearly every street anyway. There is still one road with two names and that one road which is actually three roads, but it's a darn sight better than it was.

TC6 over and out.